"Brimming with easily digested instructions and exercises, steeped in little-known historical facts, and sweetened with personal anecdotes and recipes, *Reading the Leaves* is definitely my cup of tea—and I have no doubt that it will be yours, too!"

—Dorothy Morrison, author of *Everyday Magic*, *The Craft*, and *Utterly Wicked*

"Tea leaf divination isn't just for witches: it is a natural practice that can be enjoyed by all tea drinkers. This book transported me back to my time in England, sitting in an English cottage, with a tea cup and a silver spoon. *Reading the Leaves* is well researched; however, what makes its worth and power is experience. Both Leanne and Sandra have a heritage of knowledge that has been carried in families through the generations. Their ancestors have brought forward the method you will learn in this fun and informative read. In particular, I was impressed by their chapter on timing, which is always a challenge, even for authorities in occult divination. Their method by which timelines are captured brings accuracy to readings regarding past, present, and future. I am excited to try the recipes they have included, which are a delicious way to support divination, and add to the magic."

—Laurie Cabot, author of *Power of the Witch*, *Love Magic*, and *The Witch in Every Woman*

"This book is incredible. The combination of rituals and customs of a bygone era, storytelling, and straightforward practical instructions makes this book the quintessential practical handbook for anyone wanting to tap into this ancient form of divination. The authors have successfully applied their skill and years of experience to create a brilliant and accessible handbook for everyone, regardless of experience. As I read, I envisioned how easy it will be for me to share this book with friends and coworkers who may or may not be witches. It's that universal. Although a practitioner of cartomancy for the most part of four decades, I have never been drawn to the practice of tasseomancy—until now. Sandra and Leanne instantly drew me in and made me want to put the kettle on to brew some tea and get down to the business of *Reading the Leaves*." —Mary-Grace Fahrun, author of *Italian Folk Magic*

"I was not a tea-leaf- or coffee-grounds-reader before. I am now. That's the highest praise I can give to a book that sets out to teach a technique. It hooked me with the presentation. It drew me in with clear explanation of history, theory, and method. It delivered in terms of enabling me to do the thing it describes. I am a better Sorcerer for having read *Reading the Leaves*." —Jason Miller, founder of Strategic Sorcery

"A smart, fun dive into a path of intuitive discovery. As I read, I felt like I was having a conversation, over tea, with two powerhouse psychics who prove reliable and fresh, and care deeply about my experience. Packed with useful information as well as grounded reassurance, *Reading the Leaves* is a solid resource and an awakening into new powers." —Tama Kieves, bestselling author of *Inspired & Unstoppable* and *Thriving Through Uncertainty*

"Smart, modern, practical, and witty! Thorough and thoroughly inspired with rituals, recipes, symbolism, and timelines for manifestation, *Reading the Leaves* is the definitive accessible guide to tasseomancy for our time. Wright and Marrama have accomplished something truly magickal. Like a whisper from behind the veil, they have channeled the essence of a largely Victorian occult practice and catapulted into the mainstream magickal practice of today with grace, beauty, practicality, intelligence, and wit. *Reading the Leaves* is an impressive addition to the modern magical bookshelf, honing in on the ethics of prognostication, paying homage to the past, while being completely relevant to both secular magic practitioners as well as cunning folk. Let them lead you on a thrilling dive into the psychic depths of the teacup. From establishing the conducive atmosphere for divination to choosing the perfect cup, as well as hundreds of symbols, Wright and Marrama serve the tea and keep it hot. With illustrations and explanations, *Reading the Leaves* is a must-read for advanced practitioners and newcomers to tasseomancy alike."

—Judy Ann Nock, author of *The Modern Witchcraft Book of Natural Magick*

"It is clear when first peering into *Reading the Leaves* that it is a labor of love. Its style invokes a Victorian elegance infused with a grandmother's wisdom. You can almost smell the tea brewing from the kettle as you sit in a parlor lit by dim candlelight. Leanne Marrama and Sandra Mariah Wright weave a spell throughout the pages of this book, taking the reader on a journey from ancient China into your very own kitchen. *Reading the Leaves* is more than just another guide to divination. It is a window into the magic found within the lives of these two women and the people that they have touched with their magical gifts. This will be a foundational work on the subject of tea leaf reading that will be a much-cherished addition to anyone's book collection. Upon reading this book, you will never have an empty teacup—only a doorway to destiny!"

—Brian Cain, author of *Initiation into Witchcraft*

"*Reading the Leaves* is an empowering work of divination that reveals the hidden wisdom sprinkled across the bottom of an ordinary teacup. Salem witches Sandra Mariah Wright and Leanne Marrama offer a hospitable welcome into the charming but oft mysterious world of tea leaf reading that makes it accessible to everyday people trying to make sense of their lives and provides tools of understanding using this time-honored method of foreseeing the past, present, and future. From the history of tea leaf reading to the symbols one might find in the cup, to recipes, rituals, and even communication with departed loved ones, *Reading the Leaves* bridges old-world wisdom with modern insight in what is sure to be a classic of the genre!"

—Christian Day, author of *The Witches' Book of the Dead*

"If you want to learn how to read tea leaves, this is absolutely the book for you. Sandra and Leanne are the perfect guides to this ancient and timeless practice that will activate your intuition and enrich your life. Follow their wise and whimsical advice and you'll be reading tea leaves like a pro in no time!"   —Tess Whitehurst, author of *You Are Magical*

Reading the Leaves

An Intuitive Guide to the Ancient Art and Modern Magic of Tea Leaf Divination

Sandra Mariah Wright & Leanne Marrama

A TarcherPerigee Book

tarcherperigee

An imprint of Penguin Random House LLC
penguinrandomhouse.com

Copyright © 2020 by Sandra Mariah Wright and Leanne Marrama
Illustrations by Lisa Ainsworth

Most TarcherPerigee books are available at special quantity discounts for bulk purchase for sales promotions, premiums, fund-raising, and educational needs. Special books or book excerpts also can be created to fit specific needs. For details, write: SpecialMarkets@penguinrandomhouse.com.

ISBN 9780593086551

Printed in the United States of America

Book design by Laura K. Corless

For my nana, Mary K. Fournier,
who was always there for me, and never missed a teatime.
For my mum, Joanne M. Power,
who nurtured my love of both reading and writing,
and told me I could do anything I put my mind to.
For my husband, Kevin P. Wright,
who has held so many of my dreams in his capable hands.
All my love always,
Sandra

∽

To my parents,
Rita and Edward Marrama,
who believed in the magic within me.
To my grandmothers,
Anna DiBartolomeo and Lena Marrama,
who taught me the magic of family.
Una Famiglia.
Leanne

CONTENTS

INTRODUCTION

CHAPTER 1

A Brief, Spellbinding History of Tea

Contents

CHAPTER 2

Let's Get Started! Everything You Need to Know before You Begin

CHAPTER 3

There's a Story in Every Cup: How to Conduct a Reading

Contents

CHAPTER 4

What Do You See? Revealing the Messages

CHAPTER 5

Good Things Come to Those Who Wait: How to Determine Timing in the Tea Leaves

CHAPTER 6

How Do You Know What You Are Seeing Isn't Wishful Thinking?

Contents

CHAPTER 7

Don't Panic: What to Do When Something "Bad" Shows Up in the Cup

CHAPTER 8

Connecting with Spirit, Visiting the Past

CHAPTER 9

Celebrating with Loved Ones, Honoring the Present

Contents

CHAPTER 10

Sharing with Family, Teaching the Future

CHAPTER 11

Exercises

Contents

CHAPTER 12

Our Favorite Teatime Recipes

INTRODUCTION

I s my grandmother still with me?"

"Am I going to have the money to pay for my kids' college?"

"Will I find my soul mate?"

"Should I take that job offer?"

We are professional psychics based in Salem, Massachusetts, and these and many more questions occupy the minds of our clients. They are the kinds of inquiries that are at once reaching out to the spirit world and tethered to the challenges of everyday life. Our mission is never to feed the desperate, obsessive, or unhealthy anxieties of our clients but to empower them to take control of their lives and manifest their dreams. This book is our chance to reach even more people and give them resources they can work with independently.

We've been reading for private clients and hosting public events for decades. We launched our first Mourning Tea in 2007, and have counseled thousands of people one-on-one and in small groups—people who by and large were not witches but who came to Salem looking not only for answers but for magic.

꙼

Sandra Mariah Wright

I remember the first time my mother shared my "baby book" with me; this modest collection of fun facts about the only child she would ever raise meant so much to her. And while every baby's journey has common steps, every baby's journey is entirely unique. I remember the way reading about myself gave me an odd feeling, as if the book told someone else's story, because I didn't remember the majority of what it recorded ever taking place. Some things remained true: I was still extremely verbal (I talked at nine months old), still fascinated by animals, and I still loved tea. It was the first line under the "favorite foods" category.

As a child, I spent an inordinate amount of time at my grandmother's house: my Nana watched me while my mother worked two jobs. My father was an alcoholic, and I was petrified to be alone with him because he'd drink himself into a stupor. Even at five years old, I could sense that being with him was really no better than being on my own. Luckily, my grandmother didn't have a job, so she was there for me after school and into the evenings, sometimes even overnight. Nana was very nearly born in Ireland; her mother was pregnant with her when she came over to the United States on a ship in 1911. Tea was a family tradition my grandmother carried on: she would put the kettle on at nine a.m., noon, three p.m., six p.m., and nine p.m. every day. She is the main reason tea was the first line in my baby book, as well as my first line of defense against whatever was troubling me as I grew up.

It was my father's alcoholism that first awakened my psychic ability. School was done for the day. I would be in the house with my father while my mother worked her second job, waitressing. As I walked down the hill toward home, I had a vision that he would have one of his "attacks," a physical episode where he convulsed and had to be taken to the hospital in an ambulance. I was terrified to be alone when this happened. I prayed that he would have the attack before my mother left for work. I could *see* her there, in her uniform, helping me. Sure enough, just a few minutes before she would have been out the door, my father went into convulsions, and I called out to her. This convinced me that I had a sixth sense, a way to see into the future, to sense what would happen so I could be better prepared for it, especially if it would be otherwise out of my control. This night set the course for me to spend most of my life helping others see into the future so they, too, could respond to the opportunities, obstacles, and challenges of life.

I began practicing witchcraft when I was still a preteen in junior high school. Laurie Cabot had a shop on Essex Street in Salem, and I purchased the components for my first spell there. Of course, it had to do with a boy! In the years ahead, I would come to counsel hundreds of people about their relationships. Throughout my life, the Craft of the Wise (otherwise known as "witchcraft") has provided the support I have needed to overcome obstacles, and I've had the honor of providing many others with the guidance they needed to live their best lives.

Leanne Marrama

I grew up an only child in a traditional Italian family with a few uncommon traditions. My Nana read tea leaves and interpreted dreams for her neighbors. Unfortunately, I learned very little from her before she passed away, but I believe I have her to thank for my gifts. I realized at an early age that I could tune in to people's inner lives through the sound of their voices. By high school, I picked up tarot cards and was often in the school gym playing with a Ouija board while my classmates were outside playing sports. But as graduation approached, I felt the pressure to lead a "normal" life that met the expectations of others. So I pushed my vivid dreams aside, and I began to focus on college and walking a more conventional path.

I went to Katharine Gibbs School to be an administrative assistant, graduated, and secured a dead-end job that basically consisted of pushing papers. I moved into my parents' Revere basement apartment and got married, all before my twenty-second birthday. After two lovely children and more than ten years as a stay-at-home mother, I had lost my identity—and my magic.

That is when I met my friends and mentors, Shawn Poirier and Christian Day, at my first Pagan Pride event. I was restless, eager to rediscover my magical self, and find like-minded people who could understand me. I felt an immediate connection with Shawn, and we were inseparable from day one. Shawn brought magic back into my everyday life, and I returned to my tarot cards. Shawn told everyone how psychic I was, and soon people were coming to me for readings. I started believing in myself again.

In 2003, I started working as a psychic and medium. I had rediscovered my gifts, supported by an amazing circle of people. I got involved with a local coven and proudly called myself a witch. It wasn't long before I was able to quit my day job and do readings full time. While these changes made me incredibly happy, it wasn't all sunshine and rainbows. My marriage fell apart, and I found myself in the throes of a nasty divorce. There was no turning back: my life as a typical soccer mom was over, and my children watched me transform into a full-time psychic and witch in Salem, Massachusetts.

Life as a public intuitive in the Witch City was a different social atmosphere than I was used to, and it posed many challenges. This community's waters were difficult to navigate. Everyone was positioning themselves to be top witch in the group, and I grew frustrated with some of my new friends. I looked for a deeper friendship, one that didn't rest on status. That's when I met Sandra. We were attending a ghost-hunting event for Festival of the Dead. I had heard her name mentioned with reverence and some fear. I wondered who this Sandra was and why she evoked such strong reactions. All I knew was that she had an important job with the October festival.

My friends were all drinking and following the festival owners around, trying to find the gates to the castle, so to speak. That's when I saw Sandra sitting alone, blond hair framing her face like a lion's mane. In that moment, my motivation to introduce myself and sit with her was a mixture of curiosity, social strategy, and loneliness. In the two hours that I spent talking with her, we shared more genuine honesty than I had felt in years. I came to understand why my friends were intimidated by her. She didn't seem to care what anyone else thought of her, she didn't buy into the politics, and she spoke her mind, even when it went against the popular opinion. When Shawn and Christian saw us chatting, their eyes betrayed a mixture of amusement and concern. But I was thrilled. A friendship was born.

Over the next four years, I worked hard to become one of the most sought-after psychics at the Festival of the Dead. While Sandra was a talented psychic, her ability to manage an entire stable of them was even more valuable, and so she was tasked with "herding the cats." We put together events to enlighten and entertain the tourists who flocked to Salem for the entire month of October. Our faces were plastered on posters all over the city. We worked closely together forming memories, making magic, and creating an empire.

I was finally living my wildest dream. But in the spring of 2007, tragedy struck. Shawn Poirier died suddenly. I owed so much of who I had become to Shawn, and he was gone. Once again, I found my life in turmoil. October was no longer a bright spot in my year. Instead, the approach of the Season of the Witch now caused me dread and anxiety. I very nearly left the business altogether to run back to the safety of carpooling and soccer games.

In Shawn's absence, Sandra became even more vital in helping Christian run his rapidly growing business, but their calls lacked their usual humor. When we look back today, we know we were all consumed with processing our grief. Out of that grief, we gave birth to the first Mourning Tea.

At that first tea, we encouraged our guests to share stories and photos of their friends and family who had crossed over. We believed this was the first step in healing after grief and in making connections with our Beloved Dead. We served a traditional three-course tea in the Victorian tradition. When everyone had eaten their fill, we began the readings. Sandra and I showed the guests how to interpret the symbols in their cups and delivered brief messages from the dead. We both found great personal healing in the process. I had barely been able to share my story of Shawn, but with Sandra by my side, I poured my heart out to complete strangers. This genuine act of sharing helped me open up and begin to mend. Now, when I read tea leaves for guests at our annual Mourning Tea, I know I am conveying messages that will help others who are walking through grief.

Every year, the event has grown, and we continue our mission to bring the magic of tea to as many people as possible. We have hosted the Mourning Tea, the Mother's Tea, the Holiday Tea, and the Mystic Tea for many years, and each event has a focus all its own. The power of our friendship has allowed us to do great things for others. We hope this book will help us continue that tradition with an even greater number of people. Welcome to the next step in honoring the past, celebrating the present, and manifesting a better future.

1

A Brief, Spellbinding History of Tea

How and where did the practice of tea leaf reading originate? Specifically, what's Salem's related backstory? Salem is commonly known as "The Witch City" for its connections to the infamous Witch Trials of 1692. Its motto is *Divitis Indiae usque ad ultimum sinum*, which translates as "To the farthest port of the rich East." Salem was a center of trade with East India in the late 1700s, and it was East India Company tea that was dumped into nearby Boston Harbor, starting the American Revolution.

Origins

Tea is surrounded in myth and legend. Chinese lore holds that it was invented almost five thousand years ago, when Emperor Shen Nung discovered it by chance while relaxing peacefully under a tea leaf tree. Leaves from the tree happened to fall into his cup of hot water and, as the story goes, the scent of the brew convinced him to take a chance and drink it. In doing so, he discovered the wonder beverage that we know and enjoy today.

In more concrete terms, anthropologists have determined that the tea trees growing along the lush, forested borders of Yunnan Province in China, Assam in India, Myanmar (formerly Burma), Laos, Vietnam, and Thailand are descended from those primordial groves where tea originated. From all evidence, tea drinking began here, then spread throughout Asia, eventually making its way from the Far East to the West. In these scholarly circles, the credit doesn't go to any emperor, but rather to prehistoric humans, who anthropologists theorize first sampled tea in their search for food, perhaps taking their cue from animals. Chewing the leaves gave them the energy for foraging and hunting. Once humans mastered fire and figured out how to boil water, tea as we know it was born.

By the time of the Shang dynasty (c. 1766–1050 BCE), people in Yunnan Province were regularly consuming medicinal beverages made with tea leaves and other plant matter. This is the origin of China's great herbal-healing traditions, with tea as the foundation. Later, in the nearby Sichuan Province, under the Zhou dynasty (c. 1122–256 BCE), people started drinking tea made from tea leaves alone—without any other seeds, bark, or herbs— simply to relax, or get a boost, rather than as an herbal remedy.

The practice of tea leaf reading dates back at least as far as the Ming dynasty (1368–1644 CE), which saw the introduction of the popular, palm-sized cup designed for enjoying tea: the fine porcelain *gaiwan*. Its three pieces are both aesthetically pleasing and useful: a saucer that allows the hot cup to be safely held, an angled cup with a flared lip, and a lid with a knob like a cherry on top of a sundae, effectively blocking loose leaves during drinking, keeping them in the cup and out of the mouth! This ingenious construction, combined with the ease with which shapes formed by the dark leaves could be seen against the pale interior of the *gaiwan*, paved the way for the art of tea leaf reading.

ᘒ

Another Type of Fortune Told

Fast-forward to eighteenth-century England, and the British coloni-
zation of the eastern seaboard of North America. To say that tea was
big business is an understatement: its monopoly of the tea trade
made the British East India Company (founded in 1600) the wealth-
iest company in the world. You can still visit the custom house
across from Derby Wharf in Salem, Massachusetts, today, and see
the building where the East India Company would have gone to pay
taxes to the British government on their wares. (Believe it or not, it
was common in Salem during this period to not only make an extremely strong brew, but the leaves themselves were served as a side
dish with butter and salt.)

You probably remember the battle cry from history class: "No
taxation without representation!" Many patriots denounced England's right to impose duties and taxes on the colonies, which had
no representative in the House of Commons. In protest, on the night
of December 16, 1773, sixty members of the Sons of Liberty (including Samuel Adams) boarded three ships, smashed open the chests,
and dumped the ship's precious cargo into Boston Harbor. As ninety
thousand pounds of tea hit the salt water, this act of rebellion—
known as the Boston Tea Party—became the tipping point for the
American Revolution.

❧

Nineteenth-Century Vibes

With this much focus on tea, it's no wonder the practice of reading the leaves found its way to England. Starting in the Victorian era, it became known as "throwing cups" or "tossing cups." Historian Alec Gill describes a common scenario of "a lady of the manor toss[ing] the cups after breakfast and read[ing] fortunes for her servants." (These days, it may be referred to as *tasseomancy*, *tasseography* or, more rarely, *tassology*. If you're interested in the etymology, *tasse* comes from the French word for cup, *mancy* comes from the Greek word for divination, or *graph* for writing, or *ology* for the study of a subject.)

Victorian culture still stirs up thoughts of romance and mysticism, with finely decorated teahouses popping up all over the world, and psychics reading leaves in tearooms like the nomadic Romani once did in the tea parlors of the 1800s. Victorian fashion, décor, and customs have shaped a darkly romantic subculture that is on the rise. This time period was particularly rich in customs surrounding death and grief. Between measles, smallpox, whooping cough, scarlet fever, pneumonia, and tuberculosis, many children didn't survive past the age of five. Queen Victoria's affection and heartache for her beloved husband, Prince Albert, who passed away at forty-two, didn't just consume her life—it formed the basis for the conduct, style, and traditions we commonly associate with her reign, and our own Mourning Tea is a modern tribute to this aesthetic.

⤚

The Rise of "Teatime"

We owe a debt of gratitude to the hunger pangs and assertive nature of Anna, the Duchess of Bedford, who is credited with the creation of "afternoon tea." During the Victorian era, well-to-do families began eating breakfast earlier and earlier in the day, while dinner was served later and later. This started the trend we now call lunch, typically a light meal of bread and butter served alongside meats and cheeses. But the poor duchess was still getting "hangry" long before dinner, which often wasn't served until eight. She described suffering from a sinking feeling late in the afternoon (we know it well), so she ordered that tea be served at five o'clock each day. This became known as "little tea," or "low tea," as guests were seated in the home's more casual, comfortable chairs with low side tables (hence the name "low tea") positioned close by to hold cups and plates. The afternoon tea menu of the time sounds familiar, as we serve most of these things at our events to this very day: crustless sandwiches, scones, cookies (called *biscuits*), and macaroons. This tradition became one of the most prominent rituals among the upper class.

In stark contrast, "high tea" started as a meal enjoyed by the working class (eating at the "high" dining table), later evolving into a repast that was easy to prepare for upper class families on Sundays, when their servants had the day off. British laborers didn't have time for afternoon tea, so their wives would prepare a hearty meal of pies, potatoes, bacon, oatcakes or bread, and a selection of cheeses and meats—along with a good cup of tea, served hot when they walked in the door at the end of a long day at the factory, farm, or mine. Lower class folks may only have had tea and bread, while wealthy families would serve a smorgasbord of popular indulgences like veal, pigeon (ick!), cold salmon, fruits, cakes, and one of our personal favorites: clotted cream.

You can tell a practice is coming into vogue when specialized products start to pop up, targeted to those who participate. By the turn of the twentieth century, several companies began to manufacture teacups printed with symbols for the purpose of tea leaf reading. Makers from England, Japan, China, and the United States have all produced their own versions. (We'll go over the designs in depth in the next chapter.) Suffice it to say, tea leaf reading had become popular enough to launch fortune-telling cups, which have become collector's items, fetching hundreds of dollars on auction sites today.

❧

Tea in the Twentieth Century

Tea has another association with freedom, in the form of the entrepreneurial spirit striking a blow against the patriarchy. In the early 1900s in the United States, any woman entering a restaurant unescorted was considered a jezebel, and thus the entire industry was dominated by men. So women began setting up their own tearooms, serving home-cooked meals and offering handmade items for sale . . . and sometimes providing readings to interested customers. Women were using what they knew and excelled at to support themselves—and one another—and the trend continues to this day, as the majority of psychics and their clients are women.

"Yankee ingenuity" is sometimes the result of a happy accident. Circa 1908, a New York tea importer named Thomas Sullivan stumbled into fame by inadvertently inventing the tea bag when he sent samples of tea to potential clients in small silk pouches to entice them to purchase his offerings. Instead of putting the loose tea into their pots as usual, they dunked the bags right into the hot water. It was convenient and made cleaning up a breeze. His gambit worked but not in the way he intended: they indeed placed orders, but when the tea showed up in bulk, the customers complained, asking what had happened to the pouches. Sullivan was forced to think fast. Silk was too expensive, so he turned to gauze. To this day, most tea in America is consumed in tea bags, rather than loose (but it is cut too finely to be top choice for readings).

During World War II, British soldiers and their allies consumed copious amounts of tea while fighting to defeat the Third Reich. In 1942, historian A. A. Thompson wrote, "They talk about Hitler's secret weapon, but what about England's secret weapon—tea. That's what keeps us going and that's what's going to carry us through." Tea was so vital to the war effort that Winston Churchill himself dubbed it more valuable than ammunition, and it remains a symbol of England's "Keep Calm and Carry On" mentality.

სა

Pekoe-ing into the Future

Currently, tea (not coffee!) has claimed the title of world's most popular drink, second only to water. Tea drinking and tea leaf reading are experiencing a particular renaissance in the United States. In Salem, all of our local "mom and pop" cafés serve multiple varieties of tea, and landmark tearooms offering psychic readings like Bottom of the Cup in New Orleans and the famed Tremont Tearoom in Boston, established in 1929 and 1936, respectively, are serving a greater number of clients than ever before. Tea is truly perennial. Empowering women, defeating bigots, enjoying delicious meals, and predicting positive outcomes with friends—what's not to like? Whatever you're facing, a boatload of history proves that tea can help carry you through. Put on the kettle, and let's talk about how.

2

Let's Get Started! Everything You Need to Know before You Begin

Tea creates an ambiance all its own. It smells magical, feels warm and soothing. Tea needs no help to be relaxing; it is naturally comforting. When you're alone, tea is your friend. Tea *with* a friend is even better. Tea brings people together, opening communication and understanding between friends, and sometimes even strangers.

A tea leaf reading is a ritual. It is so much more than simply drinking a cup of tea. Like any ritual, it is best performed in an environment that has been properly prepared. When we surround our senses with beauty, health, and peace, we can become more psychically fit. The atmosphere around us is the atmosphere within us.

❧

The Atmosphere: Set Yourself Up for Success

In the early years of our tea leaf reading events, the hours before we faced our guests were filled with anxiety. Our minds would race with everything that could go wrong, from the food being inedible to every reading somehow sounding inaccurate. At times, we would overhear outside the doors the chatter of skeptics waiting who seemed determined to challenge the idea that anyone was going to receive a message or a vision of the future in their cup, and it would disrupt the overall energy. When this happened, we both found ourselves working even harder to clear our minds—and the place itself—of negativity.

Inevitably, as our guests filed into the venue, the room complete with soothing music, lovely theme-appropriate centerpieces, and the scent of fresh-baked goodies, the atmosphere itself transformed any doubt and relaxed the defenses of even the staunchest skeptics. You can do this on a smaller scale in your own home. Take control of your atmosphere by tailoring your surroundings. From the physical space to the people in and around it, create a place where you can feel strong in the confidence that you are interpreting the leaves with accuracy. Here are a few rules we live by.

꩜

Banish Haters and Naysayers

If you are surrounded by negative nellies or crowing critics, their pessimism will haunt your reading and make you second-guess what you see. When you start any kind of psychic development, seek out like-minded people. Don't pay any mind to the words of cynics. If you listen to people who fear or don't believe in psychic work, you will approach your reading with trepidation, which will make it exponentially harder to receive messages or helpful information.

❦

Protect Your Privacy

When you are ready to read the leaves for yourself or with a friend, the first consideration is privacy. This factors into everything, from the choice of location to the timing. If you are worried about being disturbed, you will not be able to relax enough to receive the information. If you are distracted, anxious, or tired, you will not be able to let go and trust what you see. Carve out time for the reading that includes preparing the setting, yourself, and the items you'll need. We recommend allowing an hour from start to finish, including setup, but you may find it takes you more or less time in different circumstances. Use your best judgment when planning so you are not rushed; it's better to budget more time than you think you'll need.

❦

Location, Location, Location

When it comes to this form of divination, the "where" is a vital consideration. More than likely, you'll be spending part of the time in a kitchen or a designated area where you have access to boiling water from a kettle. Bringing the water to a rolling boil is best; the hot water that is dispensed from a water cooler doesn't steep the tea as quickly, and should only be used in a pinch. You'll also need a comfortable seat at some kind of table or desk for each person involved in the reading.

Once you've decided on the location, the next feature of a successful atmosphere for psychic work is cleanliness. Before you start working with tea leaves, make sure to cleanse the space on both the physical and psychic levels. The table should be cleared of any unnecessary objects, as clutter can be distracting to the psychic mind. Many psychics have specific items that they keep on their tables while they do readings; as long as the item supports the work at hand, it is not clutter, and it can remain.

First, wipe down or wash the table. We recommend a mixture of equal parts water and white vinegar, but test it on an inconspicuous area to make sure it's not going to harm the finish. When vinegar is not available, a bit of soap and warm water is perfectly fine. This cleansing is not only to remove bits of stray crumbs and stains from mundane meals but leftover energy from whatever has happened around that table in the past. The area in which you conduct psychic work can hold the energetic residue of countless days: If you are using your kitchen table, for instance, it could possess an aura of emotional turmoil, or just stray thoughts and feelings from conversations at the last meal you shared there. If you're anything like us, and you probably are, when your family gathers for dinner, the discussions can range from lighthearted banter to a rousing debate.

Maybe you entertained a group of your friends who were noisily eating and drinking, then an argument broke out. Or maybe you sat there nursing a broken heart. Now picture conducting a reading and attempting to connect with someone's late mother in that same space. Emotional baggage can make focusing difficult.

To cleanse and hallow the space, you might burn a substance that can banish unnecessary energy or spirits. There are many herbs that have been associated with this practice by various cultures for centuries. Cedar, lavender, rosemary, sage, and sweetgrass are all popular choices. We recommend choosing something that is grown locally, but your local occult shop will stock more exotic choices, such as tree saps like copal, Palo Santo wood, or our favorite: frankincense resin from the *Boswellia sacra* tree, combined with myrrh. Any of these are suitable, so let your nose guide you. You may also choose to use a spray if you are unable to burn things in your space. In any case, the scent of the room is a powerful trigger, and picking the right one can connect us with our memories more than any other of the senses. Our sense of smell can even be another psychic tool, making us aware of spirits around us. Many of our clients have reported smelling a lost loved one's perfume or cologne, home cooking, or pipe.

Wearing essential oils can also facilitate psychic connections. Always dilute essential oils that you intend to wear on your skin with a carrier oil like jojoba, and choose a scent that you like and you can feel comfortable wearing. Scents long believed to induce psychic states—such as jasmine, lemongrass, rose, sandalwood, and vanilla—are popular choices, as they are powerful but pleasant. These same oils can help anoint the table itself, with a drop or two in the mixture you use to wipe it down. Again, test a small area to be sure it doesn't harm the finish.

You don't have to wear the herbs to gain benefits from them. The night before doing a large group of tea leaf readings, Leanne will place a bowl filled with mugwort next to her bed to provide a psychic boost. Likewise, when she readies her space for a personal reading, she puts mugwort in a bowl near the crystals on her table to enhance her own abilities and to protect her clients and herself from any unwanted or harmful energy.

Once your space is clean, it is time to infuse it with power and beauty. When you take the time to beautify a space, you can make a regular place sacred. Crystals and gemstones on the table aid even the most practiced readers in making psychic connections, amethyst and moonstone in particular. Clear quartz is sometimes called *the master healer*, and it is known to magnify psychic power and open the mind to higher guidance. Labradorite, called *spectrolite* by many witches for its connection to the spirit world, is a favorite of psychics and mediums. This is one of the best stones for communicating with those who have crossed over. It awakens even latent or buried psychic abilities, and is like a megaphone for spirits.

Another way to create an environment conducive to psychic work is to bring in some soothing music. Cue up a playlist that makes you feel calm, confident, and open. Being relaxed raises your psychic vibration, which in turn makes you more open to messages. When we host our psychic events, we always make sure music sets the atmosphere. At our annual Mourning Tea, we have a harpist playing in the background to prepare the guests. The right song can transform a room, and set the stage for powerful messages. It can instantly influence both those who are performing and receiving a reading.

❧

Choosing the Perfect Cup

The cup is your main tool. We prefer a plain white one, especially when teaching or reading for larger groups. The unadorned cup leaves room for our creative minds to see several images in the same area. It also gives the reader more control over how the leaves can be interpreted, and does not require additional knowledge of the symbols in the pattern.

There are cups dating back to the nineteenth century that have been specifically designed for reading the leaves. Some readers prefer these decorated cups, as they provide static visual guidelines that frame the reading: that is, when the leaves interact with the designs in the cup, it all contributes to the story.

There are four styles of cups that have stood the test of time:

Figure 1: Astrology Cup

Astrology

These cups and saucers are decorated with the signs of the zodiac, which itself dates back to the ancient world. The illustrated zodiac wheel and its symbols provide a format that can help the reader well versed in astrology to interpret the timing of events, planetary influences, and aspects of the personalities involved.

Figure 2: Cartomancy Cup

Cartomancy

This style sports images of common playing cards, the designs for which can be traced back centuries. Regular, unobtrusive poker cards have long been used in place of tarot cards by readers who did not wish to be "outed" for knowing how to use them; no one would suspect anyone for having a pack of playing cards in the house. For readers familiar with the meanings associated with each, the decorated cups provide additional information through the shapes of the leaves on and around the designs.

Figure 3: Numerology Cup

Numerology

Numbers are the universal language, and they have been assigned meaning by many cultures for centuries. These decorated cups and saucers feature a sequence of painted digits, which are useful for divining dates and times but could also reference events, personality traits, or even specific people. Most commonly, numerological designs are painted in conjunction with one of the other styles here, particularly the last one on our list . . .

Figure 4: Symbol Cup

Traditional Tea Leaf Reading Symbols

Some people find it difficult to identify discrete symbols in the clumps of wet leaves strewn across the cup. These cups provide a collection of key symbols as the backdrop, and the reading is conducted primarily by seeing where and how the leaves clump on and around them.

Of course, whatever cup you choose, it should be lovingly washed before and after each reading. Many people choose to keep it separated from the cups they use every day, but it is not required. If you feel the cup should be special, set it aside and only use it for readings. If you feel that you will have a stronger connection with the cup if it becomes your favorite, go ahead and use it for your daily tea. It's purely a matter of personal preference.

⁓

Selecting the Best Tea

We've torn open a tea bag or two in our day, but the best tea to use for a successful reading is loose leaf. The tea that's packaged in tea bags is so finely chopped, it is difficult for the leaves to stick together to form shapes. Almost any kind of tea with a broad leaf will work, but we stick to the traditional oolong for our events. It is the right size and tends to form patterns with the leaves as well as in the empty space within a clump of leaves, also known as the negative space. You won't need much; maybe half a teaspoon in each cup. If you add too much to the cup, you'll end up with one big blob. In this case, less really is more.

e⟋⟍

The Mind/Body Connection

Working with tea leaves is different from working with other forms of divination. Psychics touch tarot cards and palms with their hands; some methods of divination require no touch at all. When you are working with the leaves, you are "drinking in" the reading, literally as well as figuratively. The reading consumes you; you consume the reading. Tea leaf reading goes deeper on a physical level because it becomes a part of you.

Your mind and body should be in a healthy place as well. When you engage in any psychic work, you should be well rested and in a calm state of mind. If you are under emotional duress, tired, hungry, or overwhelmed, you will be at a genuine disadvantage when it comes time to interpret. Remember, your own emotional state and what you are focused on all dictates the tone of your reading.

Hydration is vital every day, and even more so when you are do-ing psychic work. Getting and receiving readings drains parts of your body that you may neglect. A glass of cool water after a reading will help cleanse toxins from your body and spirit. Stay away from alcohol, soda, and artificially sweetened drinks, especially if you are doing readings for others. They can cloud your vision and blind you to the truth. Some will cause you to have a lower vibration, making it even harder to access your natural gifts.

ᴄᴡᴐ

What Is Grounding and Why Is It a Good Idea?

Whenever you engage in psychic work, start by making sure you feel fully present in your body, and connected to the solid, stable energy of the earth. To achieve the best connection with spirit, you must begin with a clear mind and an energized body, and you connect the two through *grounding*. When you are grounded, you are at peace in your skin. Your mind is calm (not anxious, racing, or feeling like you are floating or disconnected from your surroundings), and your body is at ease. If you are not grounded when you begin a reading, you may feel distracted, worried, spacey, or agitated.

One easy, surefire way to feel grounded is to eat. A healthy part of preparing for a reading is to make sure you have fed your body as well as your spirit, and nothing gets you connected to your physical body faster than starting up your digestive system. Food is an essential part of the tea events we host, not only because it is a common way we socialize but also because it is an effective (and delicious) way to get everyone in the room grounded. Our three-course teas begin with light, fresh scones and breakfast breads with clotted cream and berries, followed by a selection of tea sandwiches made with vegetables and healthy proteins, and end with bite-sized cookies and tarts. (For some of our favorite recipes, see Chapter 12.) The food is never excessive or heavy; overeating is not conducive to a meaningful reading either, and too much grounding can put you to sleep. It's a good idea to plan your heaviest meal of the day for after you have finished your psychic work.

There are other ways to feel grounded when food is not available or you're not hungry. The first is to take a deep breath in through your nose and push it out through your mouth. While you inhale, imagine taking in positive, pure, happy energy, and while you exhale, push out any uncomfortable, negative feelings. Feel the air filling your lungs and, as you release it, concentrate on feeling your body relaxing. Repeat three to five times.

Another technique that is especially effective when done outside is to concentrate on the bottoms of your feet, where they connect with the floor (or, even better, the earth itself). This can be done while sitting or standing. Relax by consciously releasing any tension you may hold in your neck, shoulders, wrists, hips, knees, or ankles—scan your body from top to bottom. Count backward from ten, focusing on the stable feeling you get from having your feet firmly planted.

One More Thing: A Note about Aftercare

It's crucial to repeat a grounding ritual if you feel overwhelmed following any psychic experience. If you like to carry stones and crystals, there are certain ones that can help keep you grounded through a reading, whether you are giving or receiving it: black tourmaline and shungite are excellent for this purpose. Holding a smoky quartz point or hematite stone in the palm of your hand whenever you feel unbalanced can bring your energy back into alignment.

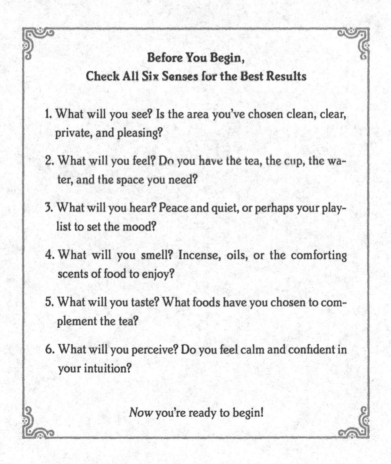

**Before You Begin,
Check All Six Senses for the Best Results**

1. What will you see? Is the area you've chosen clean, clear, private, and pleasing?

2. What will you feel? Do you have the tea, the cup, the water, and the space you need?

3. What will you hear? Peace and quiet, or perhaps your playlist to set the mood?

4. What will you smell? Incense, oils, or the comforting scents of food to enjoy?

5. What will you taste? What foods have you chosen to complement the tea?

6. What will you perceive? Do you feel calm and confident in your intuition?

Now you're ready to begin!

3

There's a Story in Every Cup: How to Conduct a Reading

The act of reading tea leaves can be as effortless or as elaborate as you wish. That's one of the things that's so wonderful about this form of divination. Sometimes we put a lot of thought and effort into the ritual, but at least as often we sit down to a regular cup of tea only to be struck with the sudden impulse to do a reading, and those seat-of-our-pants instances offer just as much insight.

ᕦᖰ

The Salem Witches' Way to Read the Leaves

What you will need:
Pot or kettle of water
Teacup and saucer
Loose-leaf tea (oolong or similar)
Notebook or journal (optional)

This Simple Method Will Show You How Easy It Can Be:

• Boil a pot of water and prepare a teacup with a light-colored interior and saucer.

> › The water needs to be boiling to steep the tea properly.

> › A white or light-colored interior will allow the images to show up clearly.

- Put half a teaspoon of loose-leaf tea in a cup—no more.

  > We recommend oolong. It's traditional (most historians agree that it was the first type of tea to be used in readings) and the leaves form better shapes than many other types of loose-leaf tea.

  > Half a teaspoon is plenty. Too much makes it clumpy and hard to see the symbols, and too little can make for a sparse reading.

- Pour boiling water over the leaves to fill the cup about three-fourths of the way.

  > Most of you won't want to fill the cup to the top when you read the next step, trust us.

- For best results, don't add milk, cream, honey, lemon, or sugar.

  > If you want tea prepared the way you like it before or after, feel free, but make a fresh cup for your reading and drink it neat.

- Steep for three minutes.

  > This allows the tea leaves to absorb the water, which will enable them to adhere to the cup and to one another.

> During this time, focus on any specific questions you have and any situations you would like guidance with.

- Drink until a small amount remains.

  > The act of consuming the tea provides a physical connection, which makes the reading that much more likely to be accurate.

  > It's vital to leave only a teaspoon or two of liquid in the cup.

  > Try not to drink the bitter leaves. Use a spoon as a shield.

- Swirl the cup in the air in front of you three times.

  > Three is the magic number, and this sets the leaves in motion. It's another way for you to add your energy to the reading.

- Place the saucer on top of the cup, with the inside of the saucer facing the lip of the cup.

  > The saucer is going to catch the little bit of liquid that is left, but it also may hold messages, which we will discuss further in Chapter 5.

- Flip the cup over onto the saucer and let the remaining liquid drain out.

> Be patient: this takes a minute or two. Continue to focus on your questions, or just maintain an open mind.

You Are Ready to Read!
Have a Pen and Your Tea Leaf Journal Handy.

• Look at the cup quickly. What do you notice first?

> Flashes of insight rule: Don't second-guess what you see. Your first impressions are some of the most potent. You may want to write them down to refer back to later.

• Examine the whole cup.

> Once you've identified your first few images, look deeper.

• Readings are a combination of lore and personal gnosis (esoteric, spiritual knowledge).

> The traditional symbols are helpful, but it is more important to make personal connections first.

༄

A Few Notes to Professional Psychics
Who Are Learning to Read the Leaves

· A psychic takes a reading beyond the lore to deliver information and messages specific to each client. The connections you make are just as valuable as any definitions you could memorize from this book or any other.

· The traditional symbols can give you clues, but the client should weigh in on the images as well, much more so with tea leaf readings than other forms of divination you may already use, like tarot.

· You will come to develop your own method that works best; no two psychics read the leaves in exactly the same way. It's a lot like cooking: start out with a trustworthy recipe and tweak it to your taste.

ல்

The Salem Witches' Way to Identify
and Interpret the Symbols

Do you remember when you were a kid, lying on your back and look-ing up at the sky? No doubt, you'd see shapes formed by the clouds. If you had a friend or two with you, you'd point things out to each other. Maybe you saw a turtle, but then your friend identified a dragon and suddenly the dragon appeared. When you were young, your imagination was strong from constant use. As you grew up, society told you that imagination was for play, and you needed to focus on work. But your imagination is capable of far more than just the games of childhood. It is still there inside you, and it is a door-way to your psychic mind. Waking up your dormant imagination is the easiest and best way to tap into your own intuition to begin receiving insight from the tea leaves.

There are sources online that will advise you to only interpret the images in the negative space between the leaves as positive, and that any images formed by the leaves themselves are negative. We don't know who came up with that, but we disagree. For more than a decade, we've been reading people professionally and that has never been the case. The majority of the symbols we see are formed by the leaves themselves, *not* the space around them, so if those shapes were "bad," we'd be seeing bad news everywhere. The leaves commonly form basic silhouettes such as hearts, horseshoes, or anchors, and those have no negative connotations whatsoever. Symbols that emerge in either the leaves or the negative space may mean blessings, or they may serve as gentle warnings about issues that will need to be managed.

The way you feel about each symbol and its history will unlock the implication, along with other factors:

- Size: larger images in the cup mean greater importance in your life

- Location: closer to the rim means closer to the present

- The presence of other shapes: how they relate and build on one another to form a story

Following the simple steps above, you can unleash your natural intuitive ability through your imagination to begin a journey of self-discovery, transformation, and empowerment, as thousands of our clients have over the years. Readings can help you make up your mind about the decisions you face, bringing validation and a sense of purpose. They can even link you to loved ones who are cheering you on from the other side, softening your grief by strengthening your connection. You already possess the tools; with guidance and knowledge, you will be able to predict opportunities, formulate strategies to reach them, and live your best life.

4

What Do You See?
Revealing the Messages

Sandra: *At our 2018 Mourning Tea, I peered into the cup of a guest who said she didn't see anything there and asked a straightforward question: "Who is J?" I turned the cup so she could see the clear, large J that had jumped out at me from the left side, and she said, "That was my mother," then choked up and blurted, "and my daughter!" She cried then, explaining that her daughter's deepest wish was that her mother would come home from Salem carrying a message from her grandmother. She looked at me in disbelief, saying, "Until right now, I never realized that both of their first names started with J. She is absolutely sending a message to my daughter. I can't wait to tell her!" We took photos of the leaves for her to show, and treasure.*

In the art of tea leaf divination, the traditional symbols are one key to unlock the messages in every cup. These shapes and patterns have a long-established connection to the concerns of countless generations of seekers, and their associated meanings have stood the test of time. Learning the implications of the most common ones can help form a map for anyone looking to navigate whatever road they are traveling.

There are several types of symbols you are likely to encounter. Sometimes, the shapes are instantly recognizable. At other times, it may take several minutes of examining the leaves before anything appears. Most of the forms you will recognize can be broken up into categories like nature, animals, objects, body parts, and numbers and letters. Through meditation, practice, and getting clear on your intention, the images will begin to appear more easily and their messages will make themselves known. The leaves will begin to speak to you.

Patterns that connect you with nature are associated with luck, which can mean blessings—or warnings. Nature is strong, free, often uncontainable, sometimes dangerous, and characterizes the basic environment you create in your life.

Animals are helpers or spirit guides. In the cup, they bring forth messages about your hopes and dreams. When you identify creatures in the leaves, you discover clues about how you see yourself in the world. Animals can help you obtain your desired future by gifting you with their wisdom and knowledge.

Inanimate objects are not formed by nature but are manifested by the will of humans. They tend to represent the day-to-day things you are doing with your life, the actions you need to take, and the energy you are putting into this world. They can have positive or negative connotations depending on what you ask and the circumstances surrounding the situation.

Sometimes the leaves look like parts of the body. This can be a reflection of your role in other's lives and how your actions impact everything around you. This can also show you how people will come into your life and create change, and what direction those interactions will take. After all, we associate certain body parts with how we interact with the world: having a good head on your shoulders or a big heart, lending an ear or a helping hand, getting a leg up, or even putting your foot in your mouth.

Numbers and letters work in conjunction with other symbols. Numbers may relate to dates, money, years, people, addresses, and pivotal memories that connect us to the living and the dead. Many people believe in the significance of seeing certain numbers repeatedly, such as 11, particularly when it shows up on a clock at 1:11 or 11:11 (commonly deemed to be a communication from angels or spirit, respectively).

At one of our recent Holiday Teas, a guest had a huge 2 in their cup. They couldn't think of a reason, so they redid the entire reading in another cup, only to see the number again. After a moment of reflection, they remembered that their grandmother's house was number 2 on her street, and her family had celebrated many joyful holidays there. Another client who was pregnant saw the number 8 in her cup. She gave birth in August of that year.

Letters can represent a person of great consequence who is coming into your life, or clue you in that someone who is currently around is going to have a greater significance. This may mean the return of an old lover, or the influence of a new boss. Letters can indicate the initial of a person's name or the first letter of a city someone who died used to reside in. Sometimes, they are a message from lost loved ones. Leanne: *I've seen the letter S in my cup more than once, which I interpret as a wave from my much-loved friend Shawn.*

It's great to understand these traditional meanings, but it's even better to be able to sift through the many layers of connotation to interpret them correctly. During one Mystic Tea at the Dunbar House Tea Room, a woman discovered a heart in her cup. Even without knowing a single thing about tea leaf reading, most people would guess that the archetypal *definition* of that symbol is love. She immediately knew it was a message from her beloved deceased mother. Her friend had a heart in her own cup, and saw it as a sign that new love was coming. Why would the same symbol mean different things for these two people? Both women drank the same tea at the same table and were very close in age, so why did each receive a separate message from the same shape? The first difference to note is the context, which is framed by each person's *intention*. The first woman had recently lost her mother and came to the tea looking for comfort. Her friend, meanwhile, was lonely, and hoping she would find a relationship soon. When they held their cups, their unconscious minds and conscious desires made a connection to the universe. While many people are open to any and all messages, if a specific question is their focus, setting the intention prior to the reading makes for a better outcome. Of course, the *position* of the leaves also plays a role in answering these questions. The heart closer to the rim and to the right of the handle indicated love approaching, coming into the present. The heart on the left of the handle was a message of love coming from the past, in this case, love from someone who had passed. Once you identify and combine *definition*, *intention*, and *position*, the symbols in the leaves become markers and messages to greet us and guide us.

☙

The Wisdom of the Ages:
Traditional Symbols for Classic Concerns

To get the most out of a reading, you must first understand the most frequently found symbols and meanings. A more comprehensive list is in our Glossary, but here are the essential ones, divided up into four fundamental categories based on the four major concerns that shape a person's life and convince them to seek a reading: love/relationships, health (particularly pregnancy or unexpected illnesses), career/finances, and communication with those who have crossed over. Keep in mind that many of these patterns are influenced by others nearby, and lend perspective on the other areas of someone's life that define the person as a whole.

Once you are familiar with these traditional symbols, you will start noticing more personal messages appearing before you.

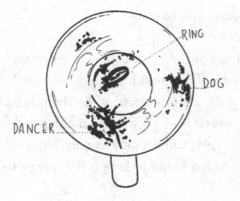

Love: It May Not Be "All You Need" but It's the Number One Thing We Get Asked About

Questions of love have troubled us since the dawn of time. For centuries, people have looked to the psychic to answer questions about finding that special someone or keeping a relationship from falling apart. What symbols should you look for if you're asking about love? Here are a few to help navigate the hills and valleys of love and friendship:

BOAT—When you see a boat, a meaningful friend or lover will arrive in your life. This is like getting a heads-up that someone is going to appear at your front door unannounced. Advance notice like this allows you to "clean house" before you let someone into your heart. If the boat appears, your ship will come in, so be prepared.

CHAIN—If you are single, seeing a chain means you'll get married after a short courtship. If you are coupled up, the condition of the chain matters: if the chain is broken, you need some serious work on your relationship; a divorce or a breakup is probable without intervention. This vital information empowers you to make changes if you hope to save the relationship.

HEART—A heart that is well-formed, with clear outlines, speaks of love. (We have seen an anatomical heart shape in the cup, with valves and all.) Combined with a circle or ring, it means engagement is on the horizon. The heart is the universal symbol for all types of love, so to read it effectively, take into account nearby symbols as well. But when the heart is not as apparent, it implies that your lover fears marriage and long-term commitment.

FAN—Fans help you cool off when you are hot. When a fan materializes in your cup, a successful romantic connection is on its way. This partnership will be passionate and fruitful. If you are in a committed relationship, this is a sign that you can fan the flames of passion and rekindle the excitement of your courtship.

RING—If you are unmarried and see a ring, it is time to start preparing for a proposal. If you are unattached and see an initial near the ring, it can predict the name of your future life companion.

BOUQUET—When you see a bouquet of flowers, good luck in romance is around the corner. A bouquet speaks to us about loyalty, meaning that your lover (or future lover) is faithful and giving. It can also indicate a future marriage filled with love and understanding.

DAISIES—Daisies bring a message of pure love and joy. They suggest that you are a person who enjoys the simple pleasures that life has to offer. If those daisies form a circle, you will attract someone with a kind, beautiful nature.

DANCER—Seeing a dancer is a wonderful message of fulfillment, and happiness in romance and friendship. True passion is dancing into your life. It can also mean that someone you love needs attention for the relationship to flourish to its fullest potential.

ANGELS—An angel is the messenger of good news. Just as Gabriel flies into the world to announce the arrival of joy, angels are envoys of happiness in love. When you see one, know that the bliss of love isn't far away. Angels bless us with news from the living and dead and want us to know affection and love are around.

BULL—This is not just a statement of a stubborn nature. If you see the omen of a bull in your cup, beware. Bulls signify that enemies are around. Take heed of drama, gossip, and lies that can be affecting your relationships. Watch what you share with others, and keep your guard up around anyone who hasn't proven their loyalty. It may be time to let some relationships go.

BASKET—Baskets bring exciting news for families that hope to grow: a new addition is coming. Families grow in many ways, so this can mean a pregnancy, an adoption, or a wedding.

DOVE—Doves mean that your relationship is filled with genuine affection, or predict the arrival of an affectionate lover. These birds of love not only speak of romantic attention but also support and encouragement from friends. Historically, doves are associated with peace, so a quarrel between lovers or friends will soon end. They are a gift of hope for the future.

DOG—Since their domestication many thousands of years ago, dogs have been man's best friend. The faithful presence of a pup in your cup means the friends you keep are loyal and true. If there is a question about your lover's honesty, a dog indicates that you can breathe a sigh of relief: he or she is faithful and trustworthy. A pooch near a heart means your relationship is more than puppy love: you can count on one another when things get "ruff."

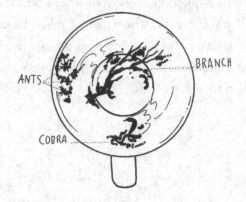

Health: What Condition Is Your Condition In?

Note: When the question of someone's health comes up, we are always careful to state that we are not medical professionals. If you see something that sets off warning bells or gives you a foreboding feeling, please contact your doctor and get checked out. Either you can stop worrying because it's a false alarm, or you can catch something early and have the best possible chance at successfully taking care of it.

The following are some indicators of well-being:

ACORN—An acorn is a message of good health. If you have an illness and want to know how you are going to fare, your health is likely to improve. Acorns are a good omen regarding all matters of healing and emotional well-being.

ANTS—Take heed if you see ants marching, as they herald illness or maladies approaching. This can also stretch to other areas of your life, as ants are a sign of imminent struggles. We have seen ants warn of broken bones that have come to pass, which is not only a health concern but a financial one as well, as breaks often lead to lost mobility and therefore lost wages.

ELEPHANT—This pachyderm is a wonderful message to find in your cup. Many cultures view the majestic elephant as a representation of health, long life, and happiness. The Hindu god Ganesh, Lord of Obstacles, is represented with the head of an elephant. When its silhouette appears, any obstacles to good health will disappear. An elephant with its trunk in the air also lets us know our luck is sound.

HEN—A happy chicken lays many eggs. When you see a hen in your cup, chances are a baby is coming.

JUG—A jug is a wake-up call that it's time to take notice of your health. If you weren't even wondering about your health, but you notice a jug in your cup, it's time to see a doctor and make some changes to your habits. Depending on the surrounding shapes, it can mean your health will take a turn for the better, or the worse, but it is always an indicator that it needs to be higher on the priority list.

Scissors—When it comes to your health, scissors are not a positive sign. Illness is lurking, and the other shapes nearby can clarify the details, like who (you or someone close to you), severity, and duration. Scissors accompanied by other symbols of discord can signify arguments, or the loss of a friend, as well.

Serpent—For many people, serpents have unfortunately been associated with negative things: sickness, bad luck, and unhappiness. Think about it: What form did the devil take in Genesis? Exactly. But what was the message? "Know thyself." Snakes remind us to listen to our bodies. When we have pain that won't go away, it's time to pay attention.

Seeing a snake in your leaves has a different resonance for members of the magical community: for witches, they are a sign of magic and the Old Gods. Leanne: *When I have read my own cup and discovered a serpent, I've squealed with excitement, knowing it was a message from a higher power. However, when faced with a serpent in a client's cup years ago, I sensed that indeed their health was in danger. I encouraged a visit to the doctor. They were diagnosed with cancer, but it had been discovered in time. They made a full recovery.*

The bottom line is, if you spot a snake and you haven't seen a doctor recently, make an appointment.

TREE BRANCH—Trees heal, protect, and feed the environment around us. Seeing a branch tells someone who is battling an illness that their good health will return. Tree branches stretch out to embrace those in need of support and give hope regarding recovery.

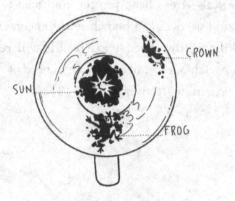

Money: It Does Indeed Change Everything

It always surprises naysayers when they learn how many professional business people come for readings. We have read the leaves for stockbrokers, business owners, doctors, and lawyers. They want advice regarding their finances, business plans, and career choices. Psychics have guided leaders in everything from major business dealings and investments to political campaigns and military strategy since the days of ancient kings seeking out oracles in wartime. When you're making your own battle plans, these symbols can guide you to victory, or warn you away from the jaws of defeat:

ANCHOR—Universally, anchors represent being held in a safe place. Here, they are symbols of strength, solidity, and success. This symbol of fortune can also indicate good luck within a partnership, including a marriage that brings much-needed financial stability. When they are upright and clear, they predict accomplishment in business. If the anchor is blurred or upside-down, you may want to make sure your job is in good standing.

APPLE—As the old saying goes, eat an apple a day and keep the doctor away. The apple often means a long life ahead, and it promises to be accompanied by a healthy retirement fund to enjoy it. An apple can also tell a business owner that they will be growing in their endeavors.

BAT—We love bats, just not in our cups. When you see a bat, it means that your current endeavors will be unrewarding. It is time to change direction, as the plans you've set in motion will not work out the way you want them to. It may be time to leave your position for another company or for another career. If you are a business owner, it is time to rethink your approach.

BIRDS—When the leaves form the shape of birds, good luck is not far behind. If the birds are flying, felicitous news is coming. If you see a bird resting with its wings tucked, or perched on a branch, a prosperous journey will shortly bring new opportunities.

CASTLE—If a castle appears, an unexpected inheritance is coming. The recipient may be unaware that they are receiving a gift, or it could indicate a sudden death. In many cases, the bequest includes property.

CLOVER—Whether the clover has four leaves or three, this is an auspicious prophecy. Even if you're not Irish, the clover's association with luck and fortune is widely known. It is always a joy to see one in a cup, because it means happiness and extraordinary wealth.

CROWN—If a crown pops up, this means success is around you and within you. You are at the top of your game and ready to become an authority in your field. A promotion and a raise, a better offer, or an award are all possibilities. Most of all, this is a sign that you rule, and it's time to own it.

FROGS—When you see a frog in your cup, kiss it! Frogs leap into your leaves to tell you of triumphs in business and love. You are ready to hop into the work in front of you and embrace the success that is your destiny.

SUN—The brilliance of the sun reveals many blessings and achievements in your career. As the sun is responsible for all growing things on our planet, it predicts abundance and growth. If you are considering starting a new chapter, now is a great time to go for it.

Moon—The moon shines down on us with opulence. If you spot it in your cup, your wealth will flourish, and your career will be fruitful, with fame and recognition followed by financial gain. Your expertise is valued, and you inspire those around you. The crescent moon is also a sign of fresh beginnings that will grow into fullness.

Star—Stars indicate big dreams coming true. The power of manifestation is yours. When you see a star near the moon or the sun, considerable fortune is coming your way.

Owl—While this bird of prey is typically associated with wisdom, if you're wondering about business, the wise thing to do is wait. Do not start any new ventures after seeing an owl in your reading. It is time to quietly observe, rather than make a decision that will lead to regret. To ignore this warning is to risk poverty and misfortune.

Worms—If you see worms in the leaves, beware. Worms warn of jealous haters who are trying to interfere in your success. They are the tea equivalent of the evil eye. Guard your finances and your achievements from frenemies.

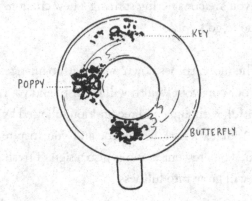

Mediumship: Hello from the Other Side

The dead attempt to communicate with the living more often than we are aware. We repeatedly neglect their messages because we don't understand the language they use. When we connect with spirit, the shapes we see are often personal to the loved one who is reaching out from behind the veil. Over the years at our annual Mourning Tea in Salem, we have often shared tidings with our guests that don't correspond to any of the traditional meanings and symbols of the leaves. Several years ago, among a table of family members who had come to honor a lost loved one, we saw an anchor in one of their cups. In this case, it had nothing to do with business or luck; it was a message from their father, who had served in the United States Navy. Not only that, they had just recently made the decision to restore his sailboat. This direct link superseded any definition in any book, and they heard Dad's message loud and clear: the old captain was happy they were taking care of his beloved boat.

Still, there are universal symbols that are widely regarded as communications from spirit:

BUTTERFLY—When you are thinking of a lost loved one and you see a butterfly in the leaves, they are letting you know that their spirit is close by, guiding you. Butterflies signify transformation and rebirth. In many cultures, they are considered the embodiment of a person's soul. When doing any kind of divination work, the sight of one reminds us that spirit never leaves us.

CROSS—As you may imagine, crosses are a representation of Christianity. When you see one in a reading, it can be a powerful message from the dead. If the spirit you seek was religious, they are signifying their presence. And you don't have to be a Christian to receive this missive, which simply says "I am with you." Crosses imply sacrifice, stability, faith, harmony, hope, and life beyond death. The spirit could be advising the living from the other side, or thanking those who sacrificed for their care.

BIRDS—Many grieving people have told us that cardinals appear after someone they love crosses over. When you see the shape of a bird in your cup, and it looks like a cardinal, your beloved dead are paying a visit. Crows and ravens are also messengers of the dead; if they appear, pay attention to the signs around you. Spirit is speaking.

FLOWERS—Flowers like lilies and roses are also often dispatches from the dead. Poppies are used to honor members of the military who have died in a war. If you see a poppy, a solider you loved is sending you a message. Often, flowers that the person loved in their lifetime emerge as a way to send a hello. Leanne: *Hydrangeas were my grandfather's favorite flowers. They grew all around his home. When I see tea leaves in the shape of hydrangeas, I know he is around.* Sandra: *For me, it's tiger lilies: my grandfather planted them in our yard when I was little, and I fell in love with their bold, bright blooms.*

KEY—A key traditionally means success in business and problems being solved around you, but when you are trying to communicate with the dead, it means the door between the two realms has been unlocked. Keys are associated with the goddess Hekate, a goddess of the crossroads and a guardian of all liminal spaces. People have invoked her for centuries when trying to contact the dead, as she presides over those restless spirits who have not fully transitioned. If you are hoping to reach someone in the afterlife, a key in your cup is a sure sign that they are listening.

LADYBUG—Ladybugs represent the human soul. Catholics believe that they live under the protection of the Blessed Virgin Mary, and symbolize her purity, grace, and capacity for love. These happy messengers let us know our deceased loved ones send their love, and that they are at peace.

SKULL—The ultimate symbol of the dead is the skull. Some tea leaf readers see it as a bad omen predicting the death of a loved one, but when a skull appears in our cup, we see it as a transmission from our ancestors. It reminds us of our own mortality, and connects us to the souls of those who have walked this earth before us. Our ancestors can teach us a great deal about the world around us and how to live; after all, without them, we wouldn't be here. If you recognize a skull, think about what your predecessors taught you while they were alive, and move forward in the knowledge that their love still surrounds you.

5

Good Things Come to Those Who Wait: How to Determine Timing in the Tea Leaves

One of the most common questions we hear is made up of this one simple word: When? In our society, patience is a rare virtue! Determining time lines for tea leaf messages is essential. We live in a world in which conventional wisdom dictates that time is precious and life is short, so it is vital to be able to forecast not only the fact that something will happen, but also the timing of it.

⌗

Basic Timing

There are many different ways to determine timing in a tea leaf reading. The most critical step is to decide what method you are using prior to pouring anything into the cup. At our tea events, we teach our guests a very simple method: symbols up near the lip are happening now, and as you move to the bottom of the cup, things are further into the future, but usually not more than a year. *Any leaves left on the saucer after the flip are read as the distant future or, at times, more messages from spirit when we are focusing on mediumship.* In most cases, the saucer only holds one, or maybe two images, which should be seen as general themes, not imagined as indicating specific events. Of course, there are exceptions, but they are rare. The distant future is not set in stone: every decision you make plays a role in it, and the more time passes, the more those decisions can alter the course of your life.

Sometimes, our guests are eager for answers and general timing isn't going to cut it. In that case, we teach them more specific methods. One such instance was at our annual Mystic Tea in 2017: A guest was determined to receive an answer that she had been waiting for regarding a new job. This person had a rather rewarding career that was cut off abruptly by a company layoff. She was fortunate enough to have received a severance package and unemployment benefits at the time, and she entered the job market with the belief that career opportunities would be coming in quickly. Instead of a flood of prospective employment openings, only a limited number of suitable positions seemed to be available. This had sent our guest into panic mode. With a mortgage and a family to provide for, she found herself in a difficult spot. She had begun to seek work in another state and started mentally preparing her family members for a possible move. Major life-changing decisions were on the table. It was July, and her unemployment benefits were due to run out in October. Time was of the essence. An interview two weeks prior to our event had not yielded any response from the prospective employer. Her question was simply, "When will I find a job?" If the answer was anytime after October, her whole family would need to move.

Once the tea was poured and the majority of the liquid consumed, she held the cup in her hands, carefully dividing it into monthly sections, as we instructed. Two images appeared clearly: a gate and a horseshoe. The guest was instantly excited. The gate represented new career opportunities being offered, and the horseshoe, with its open end toward the lip of the cup, revealed good luck in the future. Even though that was good news, the question of when mattered even more. As she visualized the division of the coming months along the wall of the cup, a sigh of relief could be heard around the room as the leaves clearly stated that a job offer would come by August. Upon further reflection, there was also the suggestion of a ladder, indicating that she would soon be climbing in her professional life. Not just a new job but a better one with more upward mobility. On Monday evening, only two days after the Mystic Tea, she e-mailed us to say she had finally heard back from the employer. They offered her the position, and she would start work before the end of August.

∾

One-Year Time Frame

If you want to examine a one-year time frame, you can hold the cup with the handle at 6 o'clock and split the cup into twelve equal parts as shown in figure 5, with the wall above the handle being the current month. Move clockwise around the cup to determine when certain things take effect or come to fruition. The closer things are to the rim, the more impact they will have, and the more likely they are to manifest in the way you desire. Things closer to the bottom require more effort.

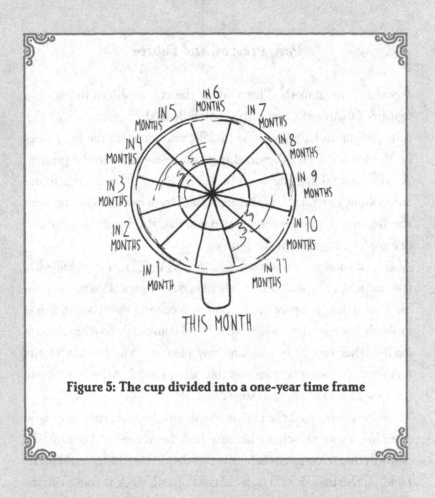

Figure 5: The cup divided into a one-year time frame

❧

Past, Present, and Future

Another general method is to divide the cup as shown in detail in figure 6. Holding the cup with the handle at the bottom (6 o'clock), split the cup in half down the middle, and focus on the lip: things on the left are from the past, things on the right are in the present. As you move down the walls of the cup, you can read the future throughout both sides. Near-future occurrences will show up near the lip, and as you travel down the walls, the happenings of the distant future appear at the bottom.

The area of *the interior cup wall directly in front of the handle* has particular significance: it is widely held that things close to the handle have a direct impact on the person receiving the reading; this is probably because that's where your hand commonly touches the cup itself. Other images in the cup may refer to close friends, family members, or romantic partners, but the ones near the handle are universally said to apply to the seeker.

Some people read the cup as one month because they like to do a reading every month, or because they have urgent concerns. To perform this reading, envision the cup divided into four equal parts. Holding the handle at 6 o'clock, the coming week is the quadrant that contains the handle, and moving clockwise, each quadrant is the following week.

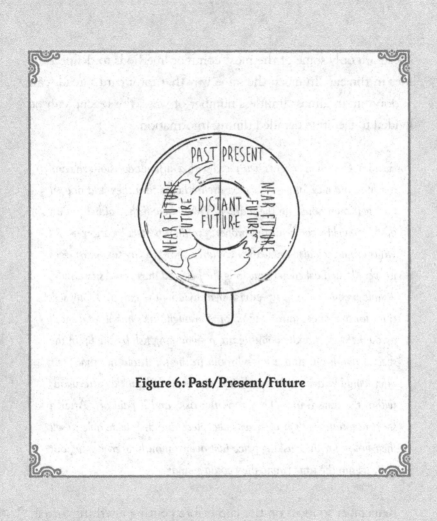

Figure 6: Past/Present/Future

⚛

These are only some of the most common methods to define time lines in the cup. In much the same way that tarot card spreads can be done in an almost limitless number of ways, the teacup can be divided to facilitate detailed timing information.

> Sandra: *One of my clients was faced with a difficult decision: she and her husband had found their next dream home, but they had not yet put their own house on the market. They knew if they didn't put an offer in quickly, the beautiful property in their perfect location would vanish, but they also knew they couldn't afford to pay two mortgages for very long. I asked her how long she believed they could sustain the double payments, and we envisioned dividing the cup into four sections for those next four months. Sure enough, the symbols of a small arrow near the handle pointing up, a swimming fish by the lip in the second quadrant, and a large broom in the third told me that their offer would be accepted, and their house would sell quickly afterward, within the time frame. They took the risk, and it paid off. After a short negotiation, their offer was accepted, and they were able to sell their house for their asking price just over a month after moving out of it, within the time frame they could manage.*

Remember to focus on the cup before pouring anything into it, envisioning the way you wish to divide it to glean the answers you seek.

6

How Do You Know What You Are Seeing Isn't Wishful Thinking?

The biggest barrier to psychic development isn't lack of ability. It's self-doubt.

Doubt is natural. Whenever we humans start to learn any new skill, we question our own abilities. Doubt isn't always our enemy: it keeps us humble and pushes us to learn more so we can become better. The challenge is to learn how to put your mind at ease so you can harness your own power.

One of our favorite parts of giving tea leaf readings is educating and empowering people to discover their own gifts. Whether people come to our Psychic Teas to see into the future, work out grief, or simply take part in a new experience, they all have this in common: they each have to learn to believe in themselves and trust their own ability in order to access information—and potential transformation—through the tea leaves.

꒰ꕤ꒱

It's Always Been a Matter of Trust

Every day we put our faith in complete strangers. When we jump into a taxi, step onto the train, or hop on the bus, we believe the driver will make sure we arrive safely at our destination. When we eat at a restaurant, we trust the chef to prepare a delicious meal that won't make us sick. How often do you trust yourself? We each possess an inner bell that naturally alerts us of danger. The question is how often we heed our instincts and keep ourselves open to psychic messages. Before we can master the tea leaves, or any form of divination, we must first learn how to have confidence in ourselves and our innate abilities.

Time and time again, we have seen our guests question what is right in front of them. They see something in their cup, but they don't say anything. Instead, they ask one of us to look. They want to know if we see what they see, and only then will they believe. Images will clearly form before their eyes and they refuse to have faith in their ability to interpret them correctly. Leanne reflects on a special moment at the Mother's Tea: *A guest asked me to review her cup. She could not believe that the word "love" was clearly spelled out in the leaves. I could see it, plain as day. I knew she must have seen it, too, as it was pretty much impossible to miss. Instead of declaring what was clearly there, I asked her what she believed was there. She sheepishly replied, "Well, I see the word 'love' and I was thinking of my grandmother, but that's way too obvious to be there that clear." In truth, I sensed her grandmother's spirit around her and told her that I felt her strong presence as well as her abiding love for her granddaughter.*

At that point, she was able to accept what she saw, silencing her inner critic.

✌

'Cause I Gotta Have Faith

We can sympathize with anyone who is feeling doubt creeping in because we've been there. We ourselves have had to wrestle with it in order to grow as psychics over the past several decades. This is especially true when we are delivering messages from beyond the grave.

Leanne: *At our Mourning Tea events, the main focus is communication with those who have crossed over. During our first Mourning Tea, I remember feeling apprehensive about certain images I saw in the cups of our guests if they seemed too bizarre, or too blatant. One in particular I'll never forget is the football I saw clearly in the cup of a guest who showed up wearing a Minnesota Vikings hat. While it felt like a message to me, I avoided it in favor of other less obvious things I saw because it seemed transparent. I didn't want her to feel like I was taking any cues from her outward appearance, something we consciously avoid so that we can go beyond the surface to access psychic information. I moved on to other guests, and she called me back over, asking me directly about the football she herself saw clearly in the cup. "My husband was a huge fan, and I thought this might be a message from him," she explained. Due to second-guessing myself, and worrying about how the information would be received, I had missed an opportunity to validate a clear message. Thankfully, the widow recognized the sign herself, and felt comforted by it. From that experience, I learned that no matter how overt a symbol is, I should say what I feel from it, whether it feels too spot-on or too far-fetched.*

Spirit often communicates in unfussy ways. The information presents itself for a reason. Go with it.

> Positive affirmations regarding your psychic gifts can help you gain confidence in your tea leaf readings. Before you even put one foot on the floor as you arise in the morning, say to yourself (either out loud or just in your mind), "I am open to receive messages from spirit. I am grateful for my gifts. Thank you." Say this not just as a prayer to the universe, but so you will hear it and believe.

Time after Time

When a symbol appears again and again, you know there's something you need to pay attention to. Repetition confirms that it's not a coincidence or a fluke. If a sign or symbol was missed during a reading, messages have a way of repeating themselves. They can manifest in all parts of our lives. At our Mystic Tea, a lovely client attended to celebrate her birthday. She was hoping for a message from her recently departed mother. When it came time to read her cup, all she could identify was a hen in her cup. Pregnancy? It did not resonate with her at the time, and it wasn't the communication she was hoping to receive. She was frustrated and pushed that image aside, hoping for other symbols to appear in her cup. Her sister and close friend sitting with her burst out laughing when they too saw hens in their cups. This guest was so confused with all these visions of poultry, she joked that Old MacDonald and his farm were sending them messages! Later, she reached out to say that when she returned home that evening, she went through some of her mother's things and noticed her salt and pepper shakers, which happen to be shaped like two hens. Within days, her daughter announced that she was pregnant. The message was twofold, and it eventually was heard loud and clear.

Repetition is a powerful sign that your messages are genuine. These symbols can be seen in different forms, and carry over from your tea leaf readings into daily life. Spirit can sneak into your dreams and nudge you for days until you recognize the significance. To separate the messages from the noise of a typical day, slow down. Look and listen deliberately to what surrounds you. Pay attention to the patterns. Divination can come from that song that seems to be on every time you turn on your radio. Numbers seen over and over again, such as dates, addresses, and phone numbers, are commonly linked to psychic information. We have many clients who identify specific personal symbols that they associate with loved ones who have crossed over. Some of them are more common than others: pennies appearing on the sidewalk, feathers showing up on the ground nearby, cardinals in a tree outside the window . . . the list goes on. These images can find their way into the cup, and they are not usually found in the list of common symbols, but that's okay. They are just as valid. It is not by chance that a guest was greeted by a butterfly while walking into the Hawthorne Hotel to attend the Mourning Tea, and then the image appeared in their cup. That kind of tap on the shoulder from the spirit world goes a long way toward validating your gifts. When you learn how to recognize the gentle voice of the universe, you will know it whenever you hear it.

❧

Write This Down

If you are seeing the same symbols over and over again, make note. Literally. Many things take time to manifest, and the only way to accurately track patterns and get better at identifying them is to keep records. Suspend disbelief and be open to the possibility that even if you see something that doesn't make sense now, it may be a clue to something in the future. This is one of several reasons why it is vital to keep a tea leaf reading journal.

Keeping a record of your readings will help you develop confidence in your ability, and help you grow in that ability. If you can review what you have done correctly, you will develop trust in your messages. Reflecting on past readings also helps us recognize what we need to work on. Writing down the information while it is fresh is imperative because it is easy to forget things we don't instantly distinguish, which can mean missing key details that become clear with the benefit of time.

Immediately Following a Reading, Record Your Results.
Here Are Some Things You'll Want to Include in Your Notes:

- Date and time of the reading, and general conditions, like weather, as well as personal status. (Tired? Hungry? Anxious?)

- Who was the reading for, and who performed it? (In the beginning, you'll probably be doing the readings for yourself, but if you decide to read for someone else, note it.)

- What prompted the reading? What was the main reason, and are there any additional concerns? Is a big decision looming? Briefly describe whatever situations are relevant. Also record any specific questions this reading should answer.

- What symbols were seen, and what are the common definitions of them? Refer to the Glossary and make note of the traditional meanings of what you see in the leaves.

- What are your thoughts, impressions, and ideas about the symbols and how they relate? Are there images that have specific personal meaning for you, and what do you think they are indicating?

- What is the overall message in the cup?

- How could the wisdom in this reading apply to the current situation?

Self-confidence is often born of practice. It is common, especially in the beginning, to discover that the symbols seen were correct, but the interpretations needed adjustment. Like all forms of divination, tea leaf reading is not an exact science. Do not discredit your gift if your teacup doesn't reveal every nuance of a situation. If you can get into the habit of documenting your readings and reviewing them as things come to pass, you will begin to see how accurate your interpretations truly are, and your ability, along with your faith and trust, will grow.

7

Don't Panic: What to Do When Something "Bad" Shows Up in the Cup

Many forms of divination can intimidate the novice seeker. Tarot cards, runes, bones, and mediumship sometimes frighten people looking for spiritual guidance. Tea offers the hesitant a more comfortable method of prophecy. The antioxidant beverage itself has healing properties; in any case, it is always soothing to sit and talk over a cuppa. Tea creates a space where we are naturally comfortable, sharing a familiar, pleasant ritual, and tea leaf readings allow us to partake in a psychic experience with very little cause for anxiety.

But even the most low-key tea leaf reading cannot guarantee good news. Not every message you receive from spirit is going to be an agreeable one. When a client greets us with "Don't tell me anything bad," we cringe. Divination is like reading a map. How can you find the most convenient and sheltered road to travel on if you are not aware of the dangers and the difficulties ahead? As psychics, we have to be able to communicate life's unpleasantries to unwilling ears. You may not want to hear what the leaves are saying because you have preconceived notions about how the future should look. A reading can give you a different perspective; a truly successful one will help you navigate upcoming turbulence and guide you past obstacles that are keeping you from living your best life.

Leanne: *Today, I am open to all kinds of truth and mystical invention, but I remember a time when I couldn't stomach anything that went against my "life plan." I was engaged at nineteen; by twenty, I was planning a wedding. When the other women at work were* considering getting tea leaf readings, I wasn't interested. My future was to get married, take a trip, buy a house, and have a baby, in that order.

But I eventually relented and joined them at one of America's oldest salons, the Tremont Tearoom in Boston. It smelled like incense blended with cigarette smoke and musty perfume. There was a pile of sandwiches, as promised. My spirits lifted. I was ready to be entertained. "Let's see if this is real," I thought as I took off my engagement ring. (Yeah, I was a jerk.)

The reading began with the psychic describing the angels around me and the power I possessed. She then correctly identified that I was an only child, which began to earn my trust. When she saw my upcoming marriage, I was overjoyed. This was real! She predicted our island vacation, and a "rich man's" family in our future: a boy and a girl. My fiancé was going to graduate college. I was beaming; all my dreams would come true.

Then things took a turn. I wasn't going to buy my dream house in New Hampshire. Apparently, I would not move out of my childhood home until I was much older. I would open my own business but struggle in my thirties; in fact, tragedy would rock my life. But she looked pleased to tell me that in my forties, I would thrive. At twenty, this was not a comforting thought. I wasn't keen on waiting twenty more years for things to get going! Then came the real bomb. She told me I was going to be married twice. As she described the soul mate that I would meet, my mind raced. Soul mate?! I was about to marry my soul mate! At this point, she could have told me the winning lottery numbers, and I wouldn't have heard anything but my own inner panic.

She promised me that the future is malleable—but she still suggested that I not get married so young. I left angry and annoyed and tried to put her visions out of mind. The only thing I wanted to remember from that day was the sandwiches. (They were very good.)

Well. Everything fell apart in my early thirties, which included a painful divorce. I think about how different my life would be if I had taken her advice and waited to get married. I realize now that while I didn't want to hear her messages because they didn't line up with what I thought I wanted, I ended up happy anyway, and I wouldn't change a thing. My forties have been the best time of my life. I live with my two kids—yes, a girl and a boy. My dream house has yet to manifest; I live in the same house that I did on the day of that reading. The second marriage hasn't happened yet, but we have been living together for ten years. He swears I am delaying the engagement to prove an old woman wrong.

Our advice is to keep an open mind, and don't reject a message because it doesn't align with your ideas about how the future should look. Life has a way of turning out for the best, even if we couldn't have imagined the road we took to get there. If a symbol comes up that has a negative association, don't panic. Instead, remember that you have the power to change the future. Your reaction to the information you receive, your decisions, and your actions all have an impact on how things turn out.

❧

The Scariest Questions Psychics Hear, and How to Respond

We rarely see folks who immediately ask, "When am I going to die?" or "How am I going to die?" In fact, most of our clients say they don't want to know. They are afraid to even think about it. When we are faced with bold seekers who are anxious about their deaths, though, we ask them to rephrase their queries. Over the years, we have discovered that if you ask the cup for aid, it will give you the information you need to actualize the life you want. Instead of asking, "How am I going to die," ask "What can I do to extend my life?"

Leanne: *During one Mystic Tea, a guest had a cup display a broken heart next to what I perceived as an hourglass. I thought, "Your time is almost up—act now, or you are going to have a heart attack!" But I would never say something so alarming to any client. Instead, I calmly and firmly said, "You may want to focus on your health. It's time for you to get into the doctor's office." I was happy to learn that she decided to take an active part in her own health; she went to the doctor, who discovered a heart issue and treated her for it successfully. She returned to the following year's Mystic Tea, and the message in her new reading was loud and clear: the broken heart and hourglass were gone, replaced by a ship and a bird, meaning she was going to travel and have good luck.*

We don't often see major warnings about health when we have not been specifically asked to address it, but when we do, we remember these guidelines, which are good rules of thumb anytime you have to deliver a difficult message:

1. Be confident.

2. Be patient.

3. Be compassionate.

4. Trust your intuition.

One of the most meaningful messages we can convey as psychics is hope. Clients do not always want to hear what the leaves are telling them, but they feel better when we remind them that the future is not set in stone. Each new day is a chance for each of us to pour a fresh cup of tea, and make changes that will bring us all closer to our goals.

8

Connecting with Spirit, Visiting the Past

We are surrounded by spirit: that spark inside of each of us that many call a soul is connected to every other living thing, and that part of us never dies. Mediumship is the act of communicating with that essence. We all have the ability to speak with the dead, but most people feel like it is a one-way conversation. The thing is, it's not the type of dialogue you and I might have in real time; once a person has crossed over, your expectations and method of communication must adjust.

Leanne: *I am the conduit for messages from my clients' friends and family members who are no longer living. During a mediumship reading, I often communicate with my own ancestors, and they help me deliver those messages. Until I met Sandra, I had never met another person who saw tea leaf reading as an effective way to speak with the dead. In fact, when we decided to write this book, we actively searched online for others who may be using a similar method and came up empty. It truly is the Salem Witches' way.*

My favorite memory of a Mourning Tea, which we hold every October, comes from one guest and her disenchanted daughter. This young woman turned her nose up at the fabulous food, wasn't impressed by the music, and refused to join others in speaking of her dead. She looked at me defiantly and proclaimed, "I hate tea." I sighed (silently) and instructed her to drink. Meanwhile, her mother loudly narrated the whole experience, saying, "Nana will come through," which was a promise that shouldn't have been made. The daughter drank her tea down and performed the ritual properly, following my instructions. Finally, the shapes were visible in the cup.

I saw a cat. Clear as day, it was a cat—an actual cat that had once existed, not just the image symbolizing something else. I was afraid to say what I saw and validate this bitter kid by telling her there is a cat in her cup instead of a loving message from her grandmother. I mustered up my courage. "You've got a cat in your cup. Your cat is at peace." I added, "Don't be angry. She didn't mean to leave before this trip." I didn't get another word out before the young woman burst into tears. Her cat had died a couple of days before their journey to Salem, and she had been in deep grief. It wasn't her grandmother, but it was exactly what she needed to hear to heal her heart.

Every event we hold reveals more wisdom. During that Mourning Tea, this grieving girl reminded us to trust ourselves. The messages that come through are not always what our clients want to hear or what we want to tell them, but what you see in the cup is what you, and they, need most in that moment.

‿

The Ritual of Tea Leaf Mediumship

Teatime is the one moment of the day when all the elements join to form sacred space.

Leanne: *When I drink a cup of tea, I am transported to a place of peace: the earthy herbs, beautiful in the white cup, while fire boils the water and the aroma perfumes the air. When I breathe in the magical mixture, I am ready to connect to the land of the dead.*

Mediumship with tea leaf readings is different from an ordinary reading with tea leaves or a reading with an evidential medium. Evidential mediumship gives physical descriptions, characteristics, names, and dates of the deceased as part of the reading. It is different from any cup of tea you have ever shared with someone. This is tea for the dead. Atmosphere is vital. Music will help you reach a deeper level of consciousness, and the songs that connected you in life will connect you beyond death. Photographs also stir the cauldron of memory and help focus the mind on who you are trying to reach.

You can follow the instructions in Chapter 2 but with two white cups and saucers. Prepare the first however you enjoy it. Prepare another plain and *set a place for your dearly departed friend or relative.* On the table, *include a few items they would have relished in life,* like delicious treats you would have shared. Personal touches make the connection easier.

As you drink, think of happy memories together. Picture those you have lost over the years and welcome them to join you for a spot of tea. Once you have taken the time to enjoy your tea, pick up the cup you set for your loved one. Drink the second cup of tea and follow these steps:

- Swirl the cup three times. As you do, visualize the person you want to invite for tea or say their name out loud.

- Direct questions to your honored guest as if they are sitting across from you.

- Take three deep breaths.

  › Focused breathing clears the thoughts of the day-to-day world from your mind.

  › Deep breathing supports relaxation and assists your life force in opening up to the spirit world.

Once your mind and soul are working together, flip the cup over and peer into its dark, leafy contents. As with any reading, shapes and symbols will appear. Look all around for images that trigger memories and reveal messages. Work quickly, knowing that your first impressions will be the most accurate. Do not doubt what you see; doubt is an affliction to all psychic work. Nothing blocks messages more than second-guessing oneself.

Pay attention to your surroundings. Understand that you are not always in control of who comes through. Don't push away messages if it isn't the original spirit you were seeking. Guidance comes in all forms. Some souls have unfinished business, so welcome them in and realize that they may help open up contact with other spirits.

e⌇ꝋ

What If Someone Comes Through
That You Had Issues with in Life?

Occasionally, unfinished business appears in the cup. Relatives, former teachers, neighbors, or others we didn't always get along with may seek to make amends or at least reach an understanding. Remember, death is a transformative experience unlike any other, and some "negative" people in our past may have a new perspective, a change of heart, or desire closure. Rather than immediately rejecting the idea that someone has taken the time and energy to reach out, accept it as a peace offering; it may help heal some of the wounds of the past.

e⌇ꝋ

Record Keeping

Over the years at the Psychic Teas, we have found photographing the cup to be helpful. You can also record your results in a notebook or journal. Often, mediumship brings prophecies and visions delivered by loved ones, key information that can help you navigate the future. Recording the results will allow you to go back and spot images you may have overlooked. You can also share them with others to hear their interpretations. Fresh eyes allow us to expand our insight and explore their deeper meaning over time.

༁

A Note for the Skeptics

Sandra: *Every year, the Mourning Tea is attended by approximately fifty guests, the majority of those women. There are always several men there who are equally interested and open to the idea of receiving messages from their dead, and then . . . well, then there are what we affectionately call "The Husbands." The Husbands are in Salem on vacation with their wives, and their wives have convinced them to attend, but they are obviously there under duress. Years ago, one such Husband sat with his arms folded and made it clear that he did not believe in what we were doing one bit. As I came around to his table, he loudly announced that he did not see anything in his cup that meant anything at all. "Do you mind if I take a look?" I asked. Right away, I started seeing the symbols, and I knew they were from a soul who strongly wanted to make his presence known. "Right here, I'm seeing a hat and a gun." I pointed. "See? I believe you know who these belong to." The expression on his face changed. Something in his eyes softened, and that tough guy exterior came crashing down. "My father . . ." His voice caught in his throat, and he clamped down again. I didn't push him to share further, but he was clearly moved that his father wanted him to know he was loved from beyond.*

The act of reading the leaves is about creating an atmosphere for meditation, reflection, and even transformation, and each experience is unique. Some of our guests may not understand the messages they receive right away, but they leave moved by the experience, and find themselves looking for signs in the weeks and months following. At the Mourning Tea, where so many people open up about their deceased loved ones and grieve openly for the first time, they are comforted by the act of welcoming their loved ones back in spirit, sharing stories that bring back happier days, and taking steps in healing, even if they don't get a distinct communiqué. Some of the biggest skeptics walking in have been our biggest believers walking out, and it's not just because what we do is real. It's also because they are afraid to risk believing. They aren't unfeeling; on the contrary, they feel so deeply that they don't want to be let down. We understand, and we encourage all of you to take the chance and be ready to tell your own incredible story.

9

Celebrating with Loved Ones,
Honoring the Present

The beautifully appointed grand ballroom at Salem's historic Hawthorne Hotel was alive with color and filled with the magical sound of a harp expertly played by a gentleman in a kilt. A riot of rich hues decorated the tables: small pots of Gerbera daisies (Sandra's mother's favorite), stacks of stickers, construction paper, and markers awaited the creativity of anticipated attendees. A new level of excitement and emotions filled us as we prepared to receive our guests. This was an entirely new experience. On this particular day, we would honor the first goddess each of us ever looked to for comfort and guidance. The first annual Mother's Tea was about to begin.

As our mothers arrived and took their seats at our table, we stood together, quietly realizing that a pivotal moment in our shared personal history was taking place. Our friend Deb and her mother joined, as well as Leanne's aunt, along with more family and friends. An old school chum and her daughter, a former colleague and her daughter as well as her mother: three generations of women, celebrating motherhood. Women we had never met came with their sisters. Some even came alone and made new friends with others of like mind. As each group arrived, Sandra's husband, Kevin, photographed them, then went to print the keepsake photos and handed them out to be used in the optional scrapbooking activity that would take place between the three courses of delicious fare.

What a blessing to see tables filled with people sharing memories with family and strangers. As each course was served, everyone welcomed traditional favorites and new flavors, scones and sandwiches and other savory treats for sharing. The crowning jewel of the day was the tea leaf readings, and it was gratifying to see so many who had never experienced anything like this transfixed by the symbols that miraculously appeared in their cups.

During the first annual Mother's Tea, and every tea since, the magic was not just in the cups but in the conversations. The laughter we heard as our mothers huddled together over their cups, discussing predictions of the future and reminiscing about the past, is a priceless memory that we will cherish forever. Beyond the considerable value of the psychic reading itself, a tea leaf reading party is a wonderful way for friends and family to come together and share an experience that will be remembered for years to come.

∽

Tea for Two, or More

There's more to a tea leaf reading party than the psychic readings . . . at least, there is when we are hosting one! The best parties involve a bit of planning. First, consider whom to invite. The people you choose to share the experience with are the heart of the event, so consider the guest list carefully. Are you looking to make new connections? A group of business associates is a great place to start. Are you reconnecting with old friends from different parts of your life? Construct your guest list with the friendliest people in your current circle, and invite a few of those friends who knew you back in the day. If you're marking a milestone, you can invite family and friends to a tea event to celebrate birthdays, anniversaries, baby showers . . . the list is endless. Once, an entire bachelorette party attended the Mystic Tea on Cape Cod. They had some interesting stories to tell!

Elegant teahouses and venues like the Hawthorne Hotel are fantastic but not necessary: you can host your own tea leaf reading party. Hosting a psychic tea party in your own home allows you to create an atmosphere and menu that invites your guests to not only take a peek into the future but also get a more personal look at your family's culinary traditions.

In cultures all over the world, food brings people together. Our home cooking is part of our heritage that we can easily share with others. The concept of "breaking bread" was built on the literal act of sharing a loaf of bread between people in an act of friendship and trust. You may choose to ask your guests to each bring a dish from their own family's treasured recipe collection. Every culture boasts some kind of tasty treat that would pair well with a nice cup of tea. And, as we have established already, tea makes everything better! If something is troubling you, a cup of tea and a heart-to-heart with loved ones will have you on the mend in no time. If you want to mark a special moment, high tea turns a modest visit into a stylish celebration.

Sharing recipes makes our personal traditions available to all, creating a bond and common ground that helps people understand one another. With this in mind, we are including a selection of recipes in Chapter 12 from our own families, as well as some generously provided by our most popular venue, the Hawthorne Hotel in Salem, Massachusetts. (Sandra: *I have friends who have been waiting decades for Mum's whoopie pie recipe!*)

∽

Magically Delicious

One of the most important things you could learn from this book is that magic is not found in some separate place you cannot access yourself. Magic is all around us, and we need only open our psychic eyes to see it. It is up to each of us to reach out and connect with the magic that can be found in our everyday lives.

As witches, we take into account the metaphysical properties of whatever we come into contact with, including the ingredients in the foods we eat. We have chosen many of the foods we have served during our own tea leaf reading parties based on what we believe the ingredients are going to help us accomplish as well as how good they taste. Lavender shortbread cookies, for instance, would be appetizing not only because they are so rich and aromatic, but also because lavender is known to increase psychic abilities. The anise in Leanne's Nana's Italian cookies is known for increasing psychic connections as well as many forms of healing. The sweet chocolate in Sandra's mother Joanne's whoopie pies is perfect for grounding energy and solidifying friendships. (Each of those recipes can be found in Chapter 12.)

We believe that blessings and power come from what we put into our bodies. The food you serve at a tea event may require very little effort to prepare and still have powerful metaphysical properties. Some of the food we serve is as humble as a selection of cheeses, fruit, nuts, and crackers, but magic can still be found in every bite. Cheese, a mood lifter and energy shifter, is sacred to the god Apollo. Cheese helps facilitate dreams coming to completion. Simply spreading butter on your bread or scone adds healing to troubled relationships. Wrap a slice of prosciutto around asparagus and you are serving magic. Asparagus has long been touted as an aphrodisiac. Prosciutto, which is an Italian dry-cured ham, is good for grounding you if you are feeling scattered.

∽

The Power in the Pantry

What other ingredients might be found in your kitchen that can be used to support your goals? We have included a list of some of our favorites for you to consider.

APPLES—Who can resist an apple? Don't ask Snow White, or Eve, for that matter! This sweet, juicy fruit is sacred to many goddesses and is believed to help with marriage, love, beauty, and the caretaking of the soul. When an apple is cut in half horizontally, the shape of a star is revealed in the middle, making it a natural pentacle, the protective symbol commonly associated with witches. You can bob for apples on Halloween, the time of the dead. Apples often are placed on ancestor altars as a symbol of immortality.

BREAD/FLOUR—Flour, when mixed with other ingredients, can create a taste treat for both the mundane and magical. Bread makes a good offering to most deities. Bread is traditionally served at the witches' holiday, Lammas, which is a celebration of the first wheat harvest. In some witchcraft traditions, charms are baked into the bread for divination purposes: handfuls of bread are torn off by participants, and whatever charm is found indicates a specific fortune.

CINNAMON—This popular spice comes from the bark of a tree. Medicinally speaking, cinnamon has been used to fight bacterial infections. The scent of cinnamon is said to bring awareness and attentiveness. When ingesting cinnamon, you boost your metabolism and your wallet, as cinnamon is traditionally used for money and success magic. Due to its accessibility and prevalence through the centuries, it is also a common component in spells for love, protection, sex, healing, and strength.

CLOVES—Recipes including cloves can promote healthy relationships and good luck. Cloves have traditionally been one of the most common ingredients in mulled wine, and are said to be a potent aphrodisiac.

CRANBERRIES—You already know the health benefits of eating cranberries, but these beautiful berries are also used for their association with healing of all kinds, as well as protection. Cranberry orange scones are always a hit at our events; see the recipe on page 158 to make them yourself.

CUMIN—This relative of parsley earned a reputation for helping to solidify romantic relationships by promoting faithfulness. Ground cumin was traditionally served in recipes to wives and husbands in hopes of ensuring fidelity. You can also place cumin seeds around your home to keep away theft and other bad energies.

DILL—Dill is not everyone's favorite flavor, but it does come magically charged. Dill can help with romance, love, and pregnancy. Dill used in food can also aid in protection and money charms. You can serve a dill pickle spear with your tea sandwiches, or add fresh or dried dill to your deviled eggs like Leanne does.

DUCK—In some cultures, duck is associated with fidelity, but one of the most notable lessons we can learn from the duck is the magic of letting go and not taking so many things to heart. We need to remember to let negativity roll off of us "like water off a duck's back."

EGGS—Eggs are a powerful symbol of hope. Frequently used to bind ingredients in a recipe, eggs symbolize the beginning of life, fertility, and rebirth. Eggs are often used as an offering to the gods of old. Many fertility spells use eggs to help bring forth life. And their association with magic doesn't end there. The shell of the egg can be ground into a powder to make cascarilla, which is used in folk magic to ward off negativity and safeguard property. Eggs can even help a person see into the future: Ovomancy, or divination using raw eggs, is a lot like tea leaf reading. Shapes that form when the egg white is dropped into a clear glass of hot water are interpreted for their significance. This method of divination has deep roots here in Salem: during the Salem Witch Trials, the Reverend John Hale testified that one of the afflicted girls used an egg white in a glass of water to determine the future husband of another girl.

GARLIC—Garlic actually does keep vampires away: psychic ones! Garlic can be found hanging in the homes of many Italian *streghe* (witches) to ward off the evil eye and prevent robbery. In terms of its health benefits, the list of what garlic has been used to treat is as long as your arm. It has been a staple of home remedies for centuries. If you are looking for an ingredient to support good health and repel negativity, it doesn't get better than garlic.

HONEY—Many tea drinkers enjoy honey in their brew. Honey, whether you put it in your tea or drizzle it over a croissant, is not just tasty—it's powerful too. Honey has been traditionally used by witches for connecting with the divine, enhancing love, building self-confidence, promoting healing, and making their protection spells stick. It is particularly potent for all psychic endeavors due to its ancient association with oracles; for example, the Greek god Apollo was believed to have mastered the art of prophecy with the help of three bee maidens, the Thriae.

LEMON—By adding lemon to a recipe, you are infusing happiness and hope to those who ingest it. Lemons have been used in concoctions to protect against the evil eye. Popular in many recipes as a digestive aid, lemon is also widely known for helping to cleanse the spirit. (Sandra: *I regularly diffuse essential lemon oil in my home, particularly in my kitchen. The bright citrus scent helps wake me up and gives me the energy to power through chores. I've also found it to be an excellent way to "clear the air" after any disagreements.*)

MILK—Milk has many magical uses, such as nurturing, protection, and success. There are various types of milk, and each one has its own specialty. Cow's milk is believed to summon encouragement, affluence, and security. Goat's milk is said to help you achieve your goals. Soy milk aids in all matters relating to work. Coconut milk can be used to cleanse the spirit.

OLIVE OIL—We both cook with extra virgin olive oil on a regular basis, not only for its medicinal qualities but also for its metaphysical ones. Olive oil has been used for protection for centuries; olive branches were hung over the door to keep out any unwanted influences, and its leaves were hidden throughout the home to keep the peace among family members. Olive leaves can even be steeped to make a tea for these same purposes.

ORANGE—Oranges are believed to bring happiness and confidence to those who eat them. They are associated with good luck, and eating them was long believed to attract friendship and wealth. Like eggs, oranges are another common ingredient that can be used in divination. As you hold an orange in your hands, think of a yes-or-no question. Split the orange open and count the seeds inside its chambers. An odd number indicates a no; if an even number, the answer is yes.

PARSLEY—This little herb, often used purely as decoration on a plate, packs quite a magical punch! Parsley brings peace in the home and protects all those who dwell within its walls. Parsley is said to give a person who consumes it extra energy, luck, and prosperity. Greeks used to decorate graves and tombs with parsley to honor the dead because it was believed to help with spirit communication.

PEACHES—They say an apple a day keeps the doctor away, but it is peaches that are believed to impart longevity. Adding peaches to a treat encourages vitality and long-lasting love.

PECANS—Pecans are used in recipes to increase material gain and prosperity. Serve a pecan dish to coworkers to impress them with your generosity—and help manifest job security.

ROSEMARY—This fragrant herb has been included in recipes to support intelligence and recall before tests, and it is said to guard against memory loss. Rosemary has been used for centuries for purification and keeping evil away. You can use the leaves in your recipes and then burn the stems to cleanse a space of negativity. It also works wonders in a purifying bath.

SAGE—In Italy there is an old saying: "Why should a man die when he has sage in his garden?" Sage is a pungent-smelling herb that protects and cleanses when it is consumed or burned. When made into a tea, sage is said to ease sore throats and help control diabetes. Add sage to your recipes to support health and wellness and banish negativity.

SALMON—Salmon, the tenacious fish that swims upstream, helps when facing challenges and difficulties. The spirit of salmon brings ideas and change as well as strength and resilience. When eating salmon, envision a positive future, and be open to receiving the wisdom you need to make it a reality.

SALT—Salt absorbs and neutralizes negativity, but be careful not to overdo it in a recipe. Salt enhances the flavors of food, but if not used with care, it can raise blood pressure. Don't spill salt while at the table or there will be a fight with a loved one. If you do spill it, take a pinch in your right hand and toss it over your left shoulder to mitigate the damage. If you are avoiding salt in your diet, another way to gain its benefits is to take a sea salt bath, which can be enjoyed to help cleanse and heal the body, mind, and soul.

SUGAR—The same way that sugar adds sweetness to food, it is known to bring sweetness to a person's life. Sugar is commonly used in love and attraction recipes. Combined with cinnamon, it can help bring money and riches. Be careful to use it in moderation; sugar can be addictive!

THYME—Thyme, an herb that increases psychic gifts, courage, healing, and strength, is a must in any kitchen. Thyme can be mixed into teas, food, and cooking oil to help with confidence and boldness to face challenges. A favorite of the fairies, it can be planted in your garden to encourage good relations with your local nature spirits.

VANILLA—One of the most popular scents to induce nostalgia and conjure memories of home, vanilla is not only widely used for its flavor but often mixed in perfumes due to its intoxicating scent. Vanilla is one of the most popular ingredients in desserts and brings warm friendships, knowledge, passion, and love. Associated with Venus, the goddess of love, vanilla-flavored treats will increase your allure by feeding the goddess in you.

⁓

Special Guests: Tea with Your Lost Loved Ones

One of the most valuable benefits of tea leaf mediumship is that it opens up discussions about grief and allows for healing and closure. Travelers have come from all over the world to celebrate the lives of those they have lost at our annual Mourning Tea. Many guests return year after year to be a part of this tradition. Some arrive dressed in traditional mourning clothing complete with gloves and hats.

They are helping to create an atmosphere of respect and reverence. When guests flow into the room dressed up in similar garb, they greet one another with a familiar nod, as if to say, "Yes, I have lost someone, too. I see you, and I acknowledge your pain." Countless times, complete strangers have taken their cup and offered it to another guest, saying, "Do you see that too?" It is heartwarming to watch people who entered as strangers leave as friends.

At our 2018 Holiday Tea, one of the guests received a personal message from her deceased Italian grandmother in the form of symbols that embodied cherished family traditions. She clearly identified the image of a fish surrounded by roses in the tea leaves. Fish is the traditional food served on Christmas Eve in an Italian household, a tradition her Nona continued faithfully. Roses were her favorite flower, and adorned her table at many celebrations over the years. It was as if her grandmother was saying, "When you want to speak with me, set the table with roses, and serve the fish I taught you how to make." The spirits of our loved ones will often tell us how to honor them and connect with them if we pay attention to the signs.

When doing tea leaf readings to connect with the dead, using old family recipes is a potent way to create a link to spirit. One of the ways you can sense that a spirit is trying to communicate with you is the smell or taste of familiar food. Bringing food that reminds us of our beloved dead welcomes them to join in our meal. This lets the people we have lost know we haven't forgotten how they gave us nourishment and love in life. Set an extra place at the table, and serve whatever your ancestors enjoyed, even if it isn't something you would expect to eat at a tea party. (Sandra: *I dare you to try to convince Leanne that Italian meatballs don't go with a cup of tea!*)

༄

Beyond Teddy Bears: Including Children

Imagine a child-sized kitchen table and chairs. Each chair holds a different character: a pretty doll in a fancy outfit complete with hat and gloves, a well-loved teddy bear, maybe even the family dog. They gather around a table appointed with a miniature tea set, and their adorable host pours imaginary tea into each little cup. Most of you reading this can picture it easily. Maybe you hosted your own tea parties when you were little.

(Sandra: *I did; I passed my little kitchen table set to my cousin Brianne when she had her son JJ. The tradition continues!*)

Tea parties have long been great fun for children. Teddy Bear Teas have become a popular event at fancy hotels, and they provide a structured environment where children have an opportunity to practice manners and self-control. The formal arrangement of a fancy tea party allows young people to experience proper etiquette, which may teach them to place a greater value on the relaxed atmosphere of the typical family gathering. Formal dressing gives kids the opportunity to put on their best clothes and gain confidence in how they present themselves. A psychic tea party like the events we host, or a private party hosted at someone's home, are a little less formal, but they offer other excellent opportunities for children to learn and grow.

As we will discuss in more detail in the next chapter, young people benefit greatly from working with their psychic gifts. Children commonly receive messages in the tea leaves easily because their imaginations are still strong, and they are not afraid to express what they see. Tea leaf reading fosters creativity and puts the focus not only on the story in the cup but on the people at the table: children and adults alike are able to disconnect from technology and allow their creative minds to explore possibilities in the shapes together. Communications and predictions aside, nothing is more magical than seeing a thirteen-year-old staring into a teacup or their friend's smiling face rather than a smartphone. That is indeed some witchcraft!

∽

Activities for Guests of All Ages

We've talked a lot about the atmosphere and the food, and those are vital components to create a successful gathering. What else can you do with your guests to help make their experience especially memorable? There are three things that have become central components of our tea leaf reading events: photography, art, and spoken word.

Worth a Thousand Words: Incorporating Photographs

At our Mourning Tea, guests are encouraged to bring photos of those they are honoring. Pictures capture a moment like nothing else can, which is why Sandra's husband, Kevin, takes photos of the attendees at so many events we host. Guests are encouraged to have their picture taken with their group. People who attend alone sometimes hold up a photo of someone they are attending in honor of, or they join with new friends they have met at the tea. The photos are instant keepsakes that encapsulate the day. At some events, photos of those who have passed or photos of those who are present are used as part of the next key activity: art.

Turn the Page: Scrapbooking

At the first annual Mourning Tea and every year since, guests are invited to participate in an art project that is akin to scrapbooking. Leanne and Sandra painstakingly provide carefully chosen stickers, stamps, and markers to adorn pages that guests decorate in honor of those who have died. The guests add photos and write personal notes to give power, love, and peace to their dead, and healing to themselves. This connects them to the energy of the people they are memorializing, which enhances the readings. They are given the option to either keep their memorial page or allow the work to enter the Book of the Dead. The Book of the Dead is a large book that houses the pages guests create during the Mourning Tea. After many years of hosting the event, there are now many Books of the Dead. This has become a time-honored tradition for both the hosts and the guests. To incorporate this into your own gathering, purchase scrapbooking and art supplies at your local crafts store, and invite guests to bring photos, or take digital photos at the event and print them out. You will be surprised at the creativity this therapeutic exercise lets loose, especially for people who don't consider themselves to be artistic.

The Power of the Spoken Word

Spoken word is an integral and poignant part of every tea event we host.

> Sandra: *This is a tradition that originated in my family with my mother, who spent decades punctuating every prominent milestone with an ode she penned herself. Every member of our family has been immortalized in one of her poems, which she would read aloud at a gathering to the delight of everyone there.*

Not everyone has a passion for writing, but most everyone can think of a song lyric, a poem, or a bit of prose that means a lot to them, or meant a lot to someone they lost. We welcome guests to share their thoughts and favorite poetry surrounding the occasion.

There's an old saying that's been paraphrased many times; the gist of it is that we die three times: once when we stop breathing, once when we enter the grave, and once when our name is spoken for the last time. When we speak of the dead, they are alive to us again. Remembering someone makes them a "member" in our lives once more. At the Mourning Tea, people stand up and share stories of their loved ones that have crossed over. This practice, typically reserved for formal events like weddings or funerals, can easily be incorporated into a more intimate gathering.

Even though the main focus of a tea leaf reading party is divination, those who attend leave with much more than a glimpse into their future. Guests are entertained and inspired through the enchanting mix of the magical and the mundane.

10

Sharing with Family, Teaching the Future

Lessons on divination, natural remedies, and countless other spiritual traditions are passed down in families from parent to child, grandparent to grandchild, and godparent to godchild in cultures all over the world. As only children, our friends are our family, and in some cases, they are now among our ancestors.

We are all born with some psychic potential, but not everyone embraces these gifts. Many brush off their second sight and call it coincidence or chance. When we are young, we don't push the impossible away. We embrace our imagination and believe in magic. Children have an uncanny way of identifying the heart of the matter; they see through phony people and fake smiles. Many are empaths and pick up on the emotions and energy of those around them. This can affect their performance in school and hinder their ability to make friends. They're simply feeling too much.

Leanne: *It's odd that my first experience of tea leaf reading came from my Nana, because we weren't close. My mother's mother had a reserve about her. She kept her emotions in check, the opposite of my father's mother, whom we all called Grandma. I wasn't sure if my Nana even liked me. After they each passed away, I cherished my memories of Grandma, and rarely reminisced about Nana.*

I had grown up hearing stories of Nana's dream interpretations and her ability to control the outcomes of her dreams. I thought very little of that gift because I did it, too; it just seemed natural. Then one Easter Sunday, after I had established myself as a psychic, my uncle came for dinner. He talked about my Nana reading the leaves and how people would come to her for advice and help. As I listened, a memory came back like a dream.

When I was a child, I loved the taste of coffee, which is what Grandma served. Nana, on the other hand, preferred tea. Red Rose—not even the loose leaf needed for proper readings. I hated it, and Nana made her displeasure with that fact known. All of her other grandchildren would bond with her over a cup of tea, but not me.

That all changed one day. I was in second grade. It was the year I changed schools and stopped going to Grandma's in the afternoon. I was not adjusting well to the shift in routine, and was desperate to avoid my new school, so I played sick. That day, Nana was the one who was available to watch me. She greeted me at the door with a serious face and no yummy treats, but she did have one thing that she promised would make me feel better: a cup of tea.

She poured the steaming water into one of her fancy cups. When I was halfway done, she broke open the bag into the cup. Gritty bits of leaves filled my mouth. I had been right all along: tea was not for me. When I put it down, she swished the remaining liquid back and forth, looked in, and said, "You are going to be fine." Then: "You'll have a husband. Children. Good." She put the cup in the sink, turned on the TV, and cleaned up while watching her soap opera.

I didn't know what that was all about. I watched TV in another room until my mother came to pick me up. Nana stopped me as I made my way down to the car, saying, "If you need to play sick and spend the day with me, it's okay. You're good company. But next time, tell the truth. Then your mother won't have to worry."

My grandmother passed me the gift, but Shawn Poirier taught me
the skill, which has become invaluable to my career. Since his passing,
whenever I teach others about reading the leaves, Shawn's name lives
on in the hearts of students he has never met.

Whatever you learn from your closest kin shapes your life and the lives of future generations. The magic of divination is a legacy that can be shared with others, and some of the best students we've ever encountered are children.

⁓

Teach Your Children Well

Psychic gifts can manifest at any age. How can you tell if a child has it? It may seem obvious, but our advice is simple: Listen, especially when they're young. It is essential not to mock them or make them feel weird. As we said, some kids with these abilities struggle when trying to connect with others, as they are typically ahead of their peers mentally. Practicing a variety of methods of divination is imperative for them to develop their skills, and not be afraid or ashamed of them. You don't have to do anything formal—have fun with it. Our friends' kids practice by looking for messages in their alphabet soup! Teaching young people to see the value in their unusual talents—and showing them that others recognize that value, too—means raising more confident, well-adjusted adults.

Psychic kids can be super sensitive to their surroundings. Loud noises, strong smells, or textures of food may elicit a strong reaction. They may appear excited, anxious, or unable to focus because of the information that they are constantly receiving. They sometimes feel so overwhelmed that they don't want to go to school and avoid crowded rooms. Other times, they can be overly affectionate and lack boundaries. With patience, guidance, and communication, parents and caregivers have the opportunity to show gifted children that being different is a blessing, not a curse. When they understand their potential and celebrate it, they are empowered to embrace the full spectrum of their talents.

Peaceful Easy Feeling

Meditation is a wonderful way for children to take control of their mental and emotional well-being. It can help return the overstimulated mind of an empathic child to a balanced state. Meditation can also help those who hyperfocus (experience periods of intense concentration to the exclusion of all else) to release their energy and receive information in a productive way. If you want to guide a child through the process of strengthening and celebrating their special gifts, meditate with them.

Begin by teaching them how to breathe mindfully. Tell them to inhale deeply, as if their lungs were balloons, and count to five in their minds, or you can count to five for them. They should hold that breath for five seconds, and then exhale, trying to push all the air out in five seconds. Have them do it three times, with the goal of creating a steady rhythm.

Once they've got that down, ask them to close their eyes. Tell them to imagine that they are sitting at a table with a coloring book and crayons in front of them, then to imagine opening the book to the first page, which has a large number seven right in the middle. Tell them to imagine coloring it in with fire engine red, then turning to the next page, which has the number six. Instruct them to color it orange, like the juice. Once that page is completed, they can turn to the next, which has the number five on it, and color it in sunny yellow. The following page has the number four on it and that should be colored in a lovely green, like the grass. The next page contains the number three, which they can color in bright blue. After that is completed, on the next page the number two needs to be colored with indigo blue, like the darkest night sky. Finally, on the last page, the number one should be colored in violet purple.

This exercise will bring them into a state of wakeful relaxation. The colors are not only the colors of the rainbow, but also the seven chakras, or energy centers in our bodies. This meditation will help children and adults alike to restore balance to their own life force, and enhance and clarify their connection with spirit. Try it just before a tea leaf reading to heighten your intuition.

Many psychic children struggle with sleep, and meditating before bed can help bring a restful slumber free from nightmares. Turn on gentle music, help them through the breathing exercise, and make bedtime a bonding experience for both of you.

ꙮ

Stop, Collaborate, and Listen

Opening up the psychic center should be done with care, especially in children, who are like sponges. They soak up everything around them, positive and negative. When information becomes overwhelming, we call it *overload*. Overload can happen to people of all ages. Irritability, anger, anxiety, and exhaustion are just some of the symptoms. Avoid overload by creating strong filters and even stronger boundaries.

1. Identify the people, places, and things that bring on negative feelings.
2. Try to determine what, if any, material reasons may be causing those emotions.
3. Respect that there may be unexplained reasons.
4. Limit contact for as long as it takes to feel good and safe again.

Children have an amazing ability to see the truth in a person or situation. If a child in your care refuses to engage with a person, don't force it. Gifted children can see past the masks emotionally unhealthy people wear. They may be picking up on someone's negativity, anxiety, or illnesses. Listen to them. Respect their boundaries so they will learn to respect themselves. Communication is key. Kids should be able to express their feelings safely, without shame. When adults listen to children, children learn to trust their own instincts. They will grow with the knowledge that they are powerful.

～

Every Day I Write the Book: Journaling

As we have previously discussed, a journal is a helpful tool for psychic development for people of all ages. An unadorned blank book can become a valuable outlet for a child to

- express their emotions and their reactions when they feel overwhelmed,

- identify patterns they notice for further research and exploration, and

- record the results of any divination to determine accuracy later.

To make full use of the journal, teach them how to pay attention to everything around them and look for any symbols that appear repeatedly. If they are always noticing a type of animal or shape, certain numbers, or other images, encourage them to write or draw it in the journal. This will help them not to obsess over messages but to record them for future exploration and discussion.

Note that children will often create their own connections to symbols and devise new ones that do not have traditional meanings but are important to them. Once, a child at one of our events saw a bear in their leaves and was convinced it was Paddington. The accepted interpretation or location of the bear aside, she was thrilled to spot a cherished friend, and felt comforted and satisfied with that, nothing more to be said. Who were we to argue? At other times, the children at our events have correctly predicted future happenings.

> Leanne: *Several years ago at one of our private events, I was reading a woman's tea leaves when her child climbed into her lap, glanced into the cup, and cried, "Oh, Mama, there is a dog in the cup!" She was confident and cheerful, and ran off to bring the news to her grandmother. Her mother sat there slack-jawed; she and her husband had just put in an offer with a breeder for a puppy. The child had no idea what they were planning, but the leaves told the tale.*

It is wonderful to watch young people take their first empowering steps toward peering into the future. When they start trusting their intuition through *any* modality, they make better choices that lead them to live happier, more integrated lives.

❦

A Cure for Teen Angst?

Once little ones grow into adolescents, communication between parents and children tends to break down. Spending quality time together creates bonds that will keep you connected even during those difficult years of personal growth. Divination is a creative way to open up a dialogue, and tea leaf reading is particularly useful because you can turn it into a meal. You can prepare it together (check out the recipes in Chapter 12 for inspiration), eat together, and examine each other's tea leaves. Certain shapes and messages can lead to deep and meaningful conversations with adolescents who are struggling with social and emotional issues. Sitting together and learning together will bring you closer and help them open up.

After a long day of school and play, children absorb a lot of drama and joy. If you are concerned that they are not behaving as usual, ask them questions about their day. Did they interact with mean-spirited people? Did they encounter someone who is battling an illness? A bath prepared with sea salt and a few drops of lavender oil can help a child relax and open up to process whatever they experienced. Nothing feels better than washing off the day's stresses and concerns.

They can also carry crystals to support them in several ways. Stones like quartz crystal and amethyst help open the third eye and, as an added benefit, amethyst will help with sleep and dreams.

Tiger's eye boosts confidence, rose quartz encourages self-respect, and blue calcite or amazonite reduces stress and anxiety and helps keep emotions in check.

❧

#Youthproblems

Some psychics we know won't read tarot for children because they don't know what to say to them; they feel that the concepts that they typically discuss are more suited to adults. That's one of the reasons why we enjoy doing tea leaf readings so much: anyone of any age can relate to the basic symbols.

When working with teenagers, we redirect questions regarding marriage and children. They have their whole lives to look for their "soul mate," which is a concern we hear more often than you might think. Questions about dating and friends are perfectly fine, but contributing to romantic obsessions in the young (or old) is not ethical. Instead, we encourage discussion about their talents, education, future career, relationships with friends and coworkers, and messages from spirit.

Leanne: *At one reading, I met a wonderful young person who was getting ready to apply for college. He was looking for a sign of where he should attend school. With a single look into the cup, he identified a huge letter E. He returned months later to tell me he had been accepted to Emerson College.*

ᴄᴀᴏ

We Are Family

Over the years, our family members have supported our efforts by attending just about every public event we've put on. We've served tea to our best friends and their extended families, as well as like-minded people we've met via social media who have become true friends, and even protégés.

Perhaps our most unforgettable event was the very first Mother's Tea. Both of our mothers were there. Together they sat, side by side, discussing the messages they each saw in the cups. Across from them was a new mother holding her baby, with her own mother by her side. It gave us goose bumps to see those three generations learning the art of divination, and making memories that will last a lifetime.

Sandra: *Thinking back to that day brings me so much joy, as well as sadness. My mother had already begun her journey with dementia, and that event was one of the last she attended. I realized that day that our roles were indeed reversing, and it was time for me to be her caretaker. The most prominent messages in our cups—hers containing a perfectly formed Salem Witch like the one on her father's police car, and mine, two hands clasped—brought things back full circle. "To protect and serve," indeed. I thought about how she had taken such good care of me by always making time, despite working two jobs* to make ends meet as a single mother after the divorce—those count-less times I had come to her for advice or a shoulder to cry on. I'd plop myself down at the kitchen table, and she'd smile her movie-star smile and welcome me the same way no matter what: "I'll put the kettle on."

11

Exercises

In Chapter 6, we discussed the benefits of keeping a tea leaf reading journal. If the illustrations on the next few pages were of readings you had performed, you would have more information to record (date, time, your status, and the like), as outlined in that chapter. Here, we will focus on what symbols you see and how you interpret them based on the Glossary in this book, as well as your own psychic feelings about the images and the stories they tell.

CUP ONE

The Intention

This person is hoping to hear about relationships, and has some big decisions to make regarding their place of residence. This reading was done using the basic past/present/future timing.

What images do you see? Note their *position* and size.

_____

_____

_____

_____

_____

_____

What are the common *definitions* of each symbol?

_____

_____

_____

_____

_____

_____

What additional thoughts come to mind when you see these symbols together?

_____

_____

_____

_____

_____

What conclusions can you draw from this reading? What advice would you suggest?

_____

_____

_____

_____

_____

_____

Did You Identify Any of the Following?

· A dumbbell at the handle, indicating new friends entering the picture.

· A turtle formed in the negative space of a clump at the bottom, signifying a stable home, good fortune, and luxuries in the future.

· Grapes in the middle on the right, with a quill pen near them; combined with the turtle, this indicates that the seeker will be buying a house, which is a solid investment. The grapes are a hopeful message indicating a future filled with richness and indulgence, and the quill pen means contracts to sign.

The Advice

The seeker should feel confident about buying a place, even if it means moving to a new neighborhood, as new contacts bring good fortune in many areas. New neighbors and possible new love interests arise from a change of scenery. This combination of symbols bodes well for job security and overall happiness.

CUP TWO

The Intention

This seeker is looking at the current situation as well as the coming year, and would like to focus on career, finances, and health.

What images do you see? Note their *position* and size.

_____

_____

_____

_____

_____

_____

_____

What are the common *definitions* of each symbol?

_____

_____

_____

_____

_____

_____

What additional thoughts come to mind when you see these symbols together?

_____

_____

_____

_____

_____

What conclusions can you draw from this reading? What advice would you suggest?

_____

_____

_____

_____

_____

Did You Identify Any of the Following?

• A bee near the handle predicts triumph and success through hard work. Bees are often a team of people that work together well as friends and coworkers.

• A purse near the top at 3 months in means profit in business.

• A large lion opposite the handle. The lion embodies strength, and can mean getting closure regarding difficult issues.

• A ladder at 8 months in, indicating that a job promotion is forth-coming.

The Advice

The seeker can count on support in the workplace from a good team, and the business is going to reflect that in the coming months. The increase in profits will translate into a promotion, and with it, a raise in pay. More responsibilities will require a show of strength, but the challenges will be met. Any health issues will be overcome (the size of the lion indicates the strength and vitality of the seeker); if ongoing care is required, the right medical team is in place (the bee speaks to the triumph as well as the teamwork).

CUP THREE

The Intention
This person is requesting a general reading; no specific areas of concern have been communicated.

What images do you see? Note their *position* and size.

_____

_____

_____

_____

_____

_____

_____

Exercises

What are the common *definitions* of each symbol?

_____

_____

_____

_____

_____

What additional thoughts come to mind when you see these symbols together?

_____

_____

_____

_____

What conclusions can you draw from this reading? What advice would you suggest?

_____

_____

_____

_____

_____

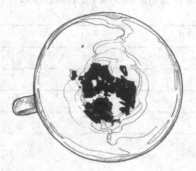

Did You Identify Any of the Following?

• Angel wings: Angels indicate that good news in on the way, and wings suggest hope, and a journey.

• Crescent moon formed by the negative space, indicating warm, loving emotions and dreams coming true.

• Seahorse with a heart formed in the negative space inside its chest, as well as a heart above it. Some cultures consider the seahorse to be a sign of good luck as well as protection.

• The heart itself is the universal symbol of love, and symbolizes trust and compassion as well.

The Advice

The seeker is entering a special time when there is much to look forward to; goals will be achieved, joy and blessings abound. No ambition or aspiration is out of reach. Full disclosure: this illustration is an actual reading we were asked to do long distance for our editor—before we met her—via a photograph she sent us of her teacup while we were in the process of writing this book, so it means a lot to us.

Leanne: *I started the interpretation, noting the angel wings and the crescent moon; our editor had seen these symbols herself, and took them as positive signs, which they absolutely are. I mentioned that blessings were on the way, and that there were exciting new beginnings coming up . . .*

Sandra: *Typically I would turn the cup so the handle was at 6 o'clock, but the photo of the cup had the handle in the position shown, which allowed me to easily spot the seahorse with the heart floating just above, and the curious heart shape in the negative space of its chest, as if its heart had popped out of it. It instantly reminded me of these frequently misquoted and famously misattributed words originally penned by Elizabeth Stone: "Making the decision to have a child—it's momentous. It is to decide forever to have your heart go walking around outside your body." I mentioned that quote and heard more than one person on the conference call gasp. Our editor was in fact pregnant, and just before we finished this book, she gave birth to a baby girl.*

CUP FOUR

The Intention

This person is out of work due to a layoff, and is hoping to hear good news about their next career move. They are interested in looking at the coming year for opportunities.

What images do you see? Note their *position* and size.

_____

_____

_____

_____

_____

_____

What are the common *definitions* of each symbol?

_____

_____

_____

_____

_____

_____

What additional thoughts come to mind when you see these symbols together?

_____

_____

_____

_____

_____

What conclusions can you draw from this reading? What advice would you suggest?

_____

_____

_____

_____

_____

Did You Identify Any of the Following?

• An arrow pointing up at the 2-month mark, with a shell in the negative space of a clump under it. The arrow pointing up indicates clear direction, and the shell is a message of good news arriving.

• A large, upright anchor 4 months in: things stabilize.

• A mushroom on the wall near the bottom in 7 months: rapid growth.

• A suitcase 10 months in with a spider next to it. The suitcase, or "trunk" as it was traditionally named, indicates a change in the surroundings: new people enter, and some people who do not add value depart. The spider indicates cooperation.

The Advice

The job hunt is successful, and the new position goes into effect in the next two to four months, with things settling down by the fourth month. Not long after, there is upward mobility indicated. In seven to ten months, a desired lateral move or an opportunity for a higher level job comes into play; it looks like a superior leaves and there is a shuffling of responsibility in the ranks.

12

Our Favorite Teatime Recipes

We love to hear our guests rave about the food we serve at our events. Some of these recipes are from our friends and families, some are from our favorite venue, and all of them will enhance your own tea leaf reading experiences.

Lavender Honey Cookies

These dainty lavender honey cookies can be cut in a multitude of shapes depending how you roll the dough. If you want to add an additional exotic hint of flavor, try using hibiscus or lemon verbena infused honey that you can find in specialty stores, online, or at farmers markets. Our friend Arianne d'Entremont Borgatti introduced us to this particular recipe.

MAKES TWO DOZEN COOKIES

1 cup (2 sticks or 225g) unsalted butter, softened

½ cup (120g) sugar

3 tablespoons (44ml) honey, any variety

2 cups (240g) all-purpose flour

3 teaspoons (3g) dried lavender (or 6 or 7 fresh blossoms, buds removed)

Pinch of salt

POWDERED SUGAR TOPPING (OPTIONAL)

2 tablespoons (16g) powdered sugar

2 teaspoons (2g) dried lavender buds

Place the butter, sugar, and honey in a large bowl and beat with an electric mixer until fluffy. Place the flour, lavender, and salt in a large bowl. Whisk until combined. Add the flour mixture to the butter mixture. With the mixer on low, beat the flour into the butter until just combined, about 30 seconds. Scrape the inside of the bowl with a spatula and fold in any flour that wasn't incorporated.

Set out two 12-inch-long sheets of parchment or wax paper. Take the dough and split it in half, placing each portion onto the paper. Form each half into an 8-inch log for round cookies or press into an 8-inch square bar for square cookies.

Wrap each log in the paper and refrigerate for at least 2 hours or overnight.

When ready to bake, preheat the oven to 350°F.

Slice the cookie logs into slices about ¼ inch thick. Place on the prepared baking sheet and bake for 15 to 20 minutes, until the edges are golden and the cookies are firm to the touch. Cool on the baking sheets.

If using powdered sugar topping, place powdered sugar in a small bowl along with the lavender and stir well. Sprinkle over cookies and serve immediately. Store cooled cookies in an airtight container on the countertop for up to 1 week.

Lavender and honey combined help create calming and loving energy with each bite, and a peaceful, loving environment for those who hand-make and serve these treats. Honey can encourage forgiveness and mend a broken heart.

Sandra's Family Recipes

Meringues, aka "Wind Balls"

These meringues made from whipped egg whites and sugar are as light as clouds. Suspend some treats inside, such as a magical combination of toasted pecans and dark chocolate chips, or any of the choices below.

(Sandra: My mother took a baking class in her college years, and she made these for my grandparents. She was particularly proud of them because they came out perfectly, light and airy and just the way the instructor taught. My grandfather took one bite and dubbed them "Wind Balls." Not exactly the praise she was hoping for! The hilarious name stuck.)

MAKES 12 LARGE COOKIES OR 2 DOZEN SMALL COOKIES

2 large egg whites (60ml)

⅛ teaspoon (1g) salt

½ cup (120g) sugar, divided

¼ teaspoon (1ml) vanilla

½ cup (50g) shredded coconut, dark chocolate chips (100g),
or nuts (40g), or a combination

Preheat the oven to 275°F. Line two baking sheets with parchment paper. Place the eggs in a clean and dry large bowl and beat with an electric mixer until the eggs are frothy. Add the salt and continue to beat until the mixture is stiff, about 1 minute more.

Gradually beat in half of the sugar with the electric mixer running. Fold in the remaining sugar with a rubber spatula, along with the vanilla.

Fold in the coconut, chocolate chips, or nuts.

Drop by the tablespoon for larger cookies or by the teaspoon for smaller cookies onto the prepared cookie sheets. Bake for 45 to 50 minutes, until the meringues are golden and firm to the touch. Transfer to a cooling rack to cool. Store in an airtight container, refrigerated, up to 1 week.

> Vanilla invokes nostalgia and softens perspective. The vanilla in these delightful cookies will bring back memories from loving friends and family. The light, airy nature of these treats can promote positive communication and joy.

Joanne's Whoopie Pies

Are they pies, or are they cookies? Or cakes? Delight your guests with some good old-fashioned sweetness with these retro New England classics. Make them in advance and chill for easier handling, or serve immediately after filling for gooey goodness.

(Sandra: *This recipe is the one people have been hounding me for forever. Make these decadent treats and you'll see why!*)

MAKES 12 WHOOPIE PIES

FOR THE PIES

1 cup (240g) sugar

½ cup (118ml) vegetable oil

1 large egg (43ml)

1 teaspoon (4ml) vanilla

2 cups (240g) all-purpose flour

¾ cup (75g) unsweetened cocoa

1½ teaspoons (7g) baking soda

½ teaspoon (2g) baking powder

½ teaspoon (2g) salt

1 cup (250ml) milk, divided

FOR THE FILLING

1 cup (128g) confectioners' sugar

½ cup (75g) shortening

1 tablespoon (14ml) whole milk

½ teaspoon (7ml) vanilla extract

1 cup (105g) marshmallow fluff

Preheat oven to 425°F. Line two baking sheets with parchment paper. Place the sugar, vegetable oil, egg, and vanilla in a large bowl. Using an electric mixer, mix on low until well combined, about 1 minute.

To make the pies: In a large separate bowl, place the flour, cocoa, baking soda, baking powder, and salt. Whisk well. Add half of the flour mixture to the vegetable oil mixture. Using a rubber spatula, gently fold in the flour mixture until just combined, about 15 turns with a spatula; do not over-mix. Add half of the milk and fold again with the spatula until the liquid is just combined. Repeat with remaining flour and milk. The batter will resemble a thick cake batter.

Drop tablespoonsful of the batter onto the prepared cookie sheets. Bake 5 to 7 minutes, until the pies crack at the top and are soft but not sticky. Cool directly on the baking sheet. While the pies are cooling, prepare the filling.

To make the filling: Place the confectioners' sugar and shortening in a large bowl. Beat with an electric mixer on medium until smooth. Add the milk and vanilla extract, mixing again until smooth.

Using a rubber spatula, fold the marshmallow into the mixture until well incorporated, about 10 turns.

Turn the pies over and evenly spread the filling on half of the pies. Top with another pie and serve immediately or store, refrigerated, in a large airtight container in a single layer, for up to 3 days.

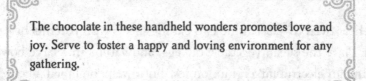

The chocolate in these handheld wonders promotes love and joy. Serve to foster a happy and loving environment for any gathering.

Irish Raisin Bread

Never made bread before? This easy Irish bread will make you look like a pro! This hearty loaf is delicious topped with flavored cream cheese and dotted with fresh berries or even freshly sliced scallions, perfect for teatime served with Irish breakfast tea or any black tea.

MAKES 1 LOAF OF ABOUT 10 SLICES

3 cups (360g) all-purpose flour

1 tablespoon (14g) baking powder

¾ teaspoon (3g) salt

¼ pound (1 stick or 110g) unsalted butter, chilled,
plus 1 teaspoon (4g) for greasing

1 cup (150g) raisins
1 cup (250 ml) whole milk
6 tablespoons (92g) sugar
1 large egg (43ml), well beaten

Preheat the oven to 350°F. Grease a 1-pound loaf pan with butter. Set aside.

Place the flour, baking powder, and salt in a large bowl. Whisk well to combine. Cut the cold butter into small cubes. Use your fingers to rub the butter into the flour mixture, taking care not to overwork the mixture or melt the butter. The mixture will be mostly flour, with pea-sized chunks of butter throughout (this will create a light, flaky crumb). Alternatively, place the flour mixture and butter in a food processor. Pulse 12 to 15 times, until pea-sized chunks of butter form throughout.

Add the raisins, milk, sugar, and egg. Stir with a wooden spoon, about 20 turns, until a soft, shaggy dough forms, and all the flour is incorporated. Form the dough into a bread loaf with a higher mound in the center. Place in the prepared loaf pan and bake for 40 to 50 minutes, until the top of the loaf has browned and is very firm.

> Raisins have been used in money spells for ages. They are believed to bring forth fertility and abundance. Bake up some prosperity magic for your guests!

Leanne's Family Recipes

Pizzelles

Delicate as lace, these classic Italian cookies will "pretty up" any teatime tray. The batter for this version is looser compared to traditional recipes, so that cookies spread beautifully in a nonstick pizzelle maker versus the antique handheld version that was cooked over an open fire in the "olden days." If you don't currently have a pizzelle maker, you can order one online for about forty dollars.

MAKES 16 COOKIES

1½ cups (180g) all-purpose flour

1 tablespoon (7g) baking powder

1½ teaspoons (4g) ground nutmeg

3 large eggs (130ml)

¾ cup (180g) sugar

½ cup (1 stick or 110g) unsalted butter, melted and cooled

2 to 3 teaspoons (12ml) vanilla

2 to 3 teaspoons (12ml) anise extract

Cooking spray

In a medium mixing bowl, stir together the flour, baking powder, and nutmeg. Set aside. In another large bowl, beat the eggs and sugar with an electric mixer on high until the eggs are thick and lemon-colored, about 4 minutes. Beat in the cooled butter and the extracts. At low speed, beat in the flour mixture until just combined.

Heat a pizzelle iron or maker according to the manufacturer's instructions and coat with cooking spray. Pour 1 tablespoon of the batter for each cookie onto the iron. Close the lid and cook for 2 to 3 minutes, until golden brown. Remove from the iron and transfer to a cooling rack. Repeat with the remaining batter. Once the cookies are cooled, store in an airtight container on the counter for up to 1 week.

> The anise in these cookies increases psychic ability and invites messages from ancestral spirits. These would be especially powerful to serve for a mediumship tea leaf reading.

Italian Sprinkle Cookies

These classic Italian treats will yield a huge batch, enough for your tea party and the family too. Dressing these cookies up with the confectioners' sugar glaze and chocolate jimmies is a kid's job and a perfect way to share family recipes (and traditions) with them.

(Leanne: I remember these as Santa's favorite cookie, wink wink! Both my Nana and Grandma baked these traditional cookies for the holidays, so they always bring back fond memories for me.)

MAKES 4 DOZEN COOKIES

3 large eggs (129ml)

5 tablespoons (70ml) mild-tasting oil, such as light olive oil, walnut oil, or sunflower oil

1 cup (250ml) whole milk

1 cup (240g) sugar

2 teaspoons (98ml) anise or lemon extract

1 teaspoon (4ml) vanilla extract

4 cups (480g) flour

5 teaspoons (38g) baking powder

ICING
¼ cup (32g) confectioners' sugar

1 tablespoon (14ml) water

¼ cup (42g) chocolate sprinkles

Preheat the oven to 400°F. Line two baking sheets with parchment paper.

Make the cookies: Place the eggs and oil in a large mixing bowl. Beat on medium speed with an electric mixer until well combined, about 30 seconds. Add the milk, sugar, and extracts, beating until just combined.

In a large bowl, whisk together the flour and baking powder. Add the flour to the oil mixture. Using a wooden spoon, mix slowly until a firm dough forms that's not sticky. Roll tablespoons of the dough into walnut-sized balls or drop tablespoonsful directly onto the prepared baking sheets, about ½ inch apart.

Bake for 6 to 8 minutes, until the tops of the cookies begin to brown slightly and are firm to the touch. Cool on the baking sheets. Once the cookies are cool, prepare the icing: Place the confectioners' sugar into a small bowl and add the water. Stir well until a thin icing forms. Drizzle over the cookies and sprinkle with the chocolate sprinkles. Allow the icing to firm slightly, about 10 minutes, then serve, or store in an airtight container on the countertop for up to 1 week.

> Add lemon to these cookies to cleanse and clear away negativity, promoting a sunny, happy environment. Energizing lemon is also used to protect against the return of unwanted energies.

Hawthorne Hotel Recipes

Cranberry Orange Scones

Traditional teatime chats would not be complete without a plate of flaky scones. Serve these simple, not-too-sweet treats at your very first tea reading party to delight your guests and make them feel at home with the magic of homemade baked goods.

MAKES 26 SCONES

4 cups plus ¼ cup (510g) all-purpose flour, plus additional for the counter

¼ cup (60g) sugar plus an extra ¼ cup (60g), for additional sprinkling

2 tablespoons (28g) baking powder

2 teaspoons (16g) salt

¾ pound (1½ cup or 350g) cold, unsalted butter

4 extra-large eggs (172 ml), lightly beaten

1 cup (250ml) cold heavy cream

1 tablespoon (14g) orange zest

1 cup (128g) dried cranberries

1 egg beaten with 2 tablespoons water or milk (70ml), for egg wash

GLAZE

½ cup (50g) plus 2 tablespoons confectioners' sugar

4 teaspoons (18ml) freshly squeezed orange juice

Preheat the oven to 400°F. Line a baking sheet with parchment paper.

Place 4 cups of the flour, ¼ cup of sugar, the baking powder, and salt in a large bowl and lightly whisk.

Cut the butter into small cubes. Use your fingers to rub the butter into the dry mixture, taking care not to overwork the mixture or melt the butter. The mixture will be mostly flour, with pea-sized chunks of butter. Alternatively, place the flour mixture and butter in a food processor. Pulse 12 to 15 times, until pea-sized chunks of butter form throughout.

In a separate bowl, stir together the eggs, heavy cream, and orange zest. Add to the flour mixture and stir with a spoon until just blended and a lumpy dough forms. Stir in the dried cranberries and the remaining ¼ cup flour until just combined, about 8 turns with a spoon.

Place the dough onto a well-floured surface and gather into a ball. Flour your hands and a rolling pin and roll the dough to ¾ inch thick. You should see small bits of butter in the dough. Keep moving the dough on the floured board so it doesn't stick. Using a 3-inch round biscuit cutter, cut out the scones and place them on a baking pan lined with parchment paper. Collect the scraps neatly, roll them out, and cut out more scones.

Brush the tops of the scones with the egg wash, sprinkle with the remaining ¼ cup sugar, and bake for 20 to 25 minutes, until the tops are browned and firm to the touch. Cool for 15 minutes on the baking sheet. While the scones are cooling, make the glaze. In a small bowl, whisk the confectioners' sugar and orange juice, and drizzle over the scones.

Chef's note: Don't pack the flour when measuring; gently scoop it with a measuring cup, or spoon the flour into a measuring cup.

> These treats pack a double whammy: oranges boost psychic gifts and bring good luck, while cranberries are perfect for social gatherings because they fill people with positive energy.

Vegetarian Pinwheels

These festive pinwheels are ideal for vegetarian guests, but they're delicious enough to be appreciated by anyone you're entertaining. For a shortcut, purchase premade hummus and tabbouleh at your local grocery store. Shh, we won't tell . . .

MAKES 36 PINWHEELS

HUMMUS

¼ cup (50ml) well-stirred tahini

¼ cup (50ml) fresh lemon juice

3 tablespoons (44ml) extra virgin olive oil

1 small garlic clove (6g), minced

2 teaspoons (6g) ground cumin

1 tablespoon (14ml) water

½ to ¾ teaspoon (4 to 6g) salt

1 15-ounce can chickpeas (garbanzo beans),
drained and well rinsed under cold water

¼ teaspoon (.25g) freshly ground black pepper

Make the hummus: Place the tahini and lemon juice in a food processor and process for about 1 minute. Scrape the sides and process for another 30 seconds. Add the olive oil, garlic, cumin, water, and salt. Process for another minute, scrape the sides, and process for another 30 to 60 seconds, until well blended.

Add half of the chickpeas to the bowl and process for about 1 minute. Scrape the sides, then add the remaining chickpeas and process until thick and smooth, about 1 to 2 minutes. The hummus may be too thick or still have tiny bits of chickpea. If so, slowly add 2 to 3 more tablespoons of water with the processor running until you reach your desired consistency. Add salt and pepper to taste.

TABBOULEH

½ cup (55g) fine bulgur wheat

¾ cup cold water

3 cups (about 3 bunches, 113g) chopped curly-leaf parsley

2 ripe tomatoes (28g), finely chopped

1 bunch scallions (120g), finely chopped

¼ cup (12g) chopped mint

¼ cup (60ml) extra virgin olive oil

Juice of 2 large lemons (180g)

1 garlic clove (6g), minced

½ to ¾ teaspoon salt (2 to 3g)

¼ teaspoon (.25g) freshly ground black pepper

Make the tabbouleh: Place the bulgur in a bowl and cover with the water. Soak for 25 minutes uncovered on the countertop, until slightly softened and all the liquid is absorbed.

Toss the bulgur with the parsley, tomato, scallions, mint, olive oil, lemon juice, garlic, salt, and pepper. Taste and adjust the seasonings to your liking. Leave at room temperature or in the refrigerator for 2 to 3 hours so that the bulgur can continue to absorb the dressing while you prep the other ingredients.

PINWHEELS

One 6-count package of 8-inch soft flour wraps, any variety, such as spinach

To assemble the pinwheels, set out the six wraps. Divide the hummus equally among the wraps and smooth with a rubber spatula within an inch of the edges. Top with the tabbouleh and spread within an inch of the edges, covering the hummus, and roll up each wrap. Transfer to a cutting board. Using a serrated knife, slice into 2- to 4-inch-thick pinwheels.

> Garlic is frequently used for protection from any negative influences. It is also said to bring passion to relationships. Cumin is garlic's perfect partner: it keeps evil and bad luck at bay and, when fed to a lover, will keep them faithful.

Flaked Salmon Salad Tea Sandwiches

Ladies who have the rare opportunity to lunch will adore these petite salmon salad sandwiches with big flavor. If you're not a fan of dill, swap it for the same amount of freshly chopped basil or even cilantro.

MAKES 32 SANDWICHES

2 pounds (900g) skin-on salmon filets
2 tablespoons (28ml) olive oil

1 teaspoon (4g) salt

¼ teaspoon (.25g) freshly ground black pepper

½ cup (118ml) mayonnaise

½ bunch of fresh dill (20g)

½ red onion (136g), diced

½ cup (100g) drained capers

Zest and juice of 1 lemon (90g)

One 10-ounce (280g) loaf wheat bread

Preheat the oven to 350°F. Line a baking sheet with parchment paper.

Place the salmon skin-side down on the prepared baking sheet. Drizzle with the oil and half the salt and pepper, and bake for 20 to 25 minutes, until the salmon is golden and flakes when pressed with a fork. Drain any liquid from the sheet pan and let the salmon cool to room temperature. While the salmon is cooling, prepare the dressing.

In a large bowl, add the mayonnaise, dill, onion, capers, lemon zest and juice, and the remaining salt and pepper. Mix well. Add the salmon to the bowl with the dressing, folding it in with a spatula so that it just "flakes," creating a chucky salad texture. Do not over-mix.

Lay out half of the wheat bread slices on the countertop. Apply an even amount of salmon salad, making sure to spread to the edges. Top with another slice of bread. Using a serrated knife, cut off the crusts and cut each large sandwich into 4 even squares. Serve immediately or cover with plastic wrap and refrigerate until ready to serve.

> Salmon is a symbol of transformation and wisdom. The energy of salmon gives people strength to move forward and fight adversity.

Caramelized Peach Crisps

These fanciful twists on crostini have the sweet and salty combo of cured pork and peaches softened by luscious honeyed ricotta. Balsamic glaze, a gourmet topping, is simply reduced balsamic vinegar that you can find online or in the aisle with Italian products.

MAKES ABOUT 15 SLICES

1 baguette (about 10 ounces or 290 grams)

¼ cup (60ml) olive oil

1 teaspoon (4g) salt

4 ounces (113g) thinly sliced pork belly or thickly cut bacon
(about 4 slices)

2 semi-ripe, large peaches (240g), thinly sliced

2 tablespoons (32g) packed dark brown sugar

1 cup (236g) whole milk ricotta

2 tablespoons (30ml) honey, any variety

¼ teaspoon (.25g) freshly ground black pepper

¼ cup (60ml) store-bought balsamic glaze

½ cup (10g) fresh basil leaves, thinly sliced

Preheat the oven to 350°F. Slice the baguette into thin ¼-inch slices; you should have about 15 slices. Arrange them on an ungreased baking sheet. Brush the baguette slices with the olive oil and sprinkle with ½ teaspoon salt. Bake for 6 to 7 minutes, or until crisp. Remove from the oven, but keep the oven temperature at 350°F. Transfer to a platter and set aside.

Line a plate with paper towels. Place the pork belly in a small, cold skillet on the stove. Raise the heat to medium and cook for 6 to 7 minutes on each side or until it begins to crisp. Once crisp, transfer to the paper towel–lined plate to absorb excess fat.

Line a baking sheet with parchment paper. Place the peaches and brown sugar in a large bowl. Toss well and spread out on the prepared baking sheet. Bake for 10 to 12 minutes, until they begin to brown and the slices are tender. Set aside to cool.

In a medium bowl, whisk together the ricotta, honey, the remaining ½ teaspoon salt, and the pepper. To assemble the crisps, spread one tablespoon of the ricotta mixture onto each baguette slice. Top each piece with a thin slice of pork belly and one slice of caramelized peach. Drizzle the crisps with the balsamic glaze and sprinkle with the basil. Serve immediately.

> Peaches are known to keep away both physical sickness and negative energies of all kinds. Brown sugar makes this protection even sweeter, promoting harmony and happiness.

Micro Yogurt Parfait

Especially refreshing in the summer, these are perfect for any time of day. You can substitute crushed cereal or cookies for the granola as a matter of personal taste, or in a pinch if you don't have granola on hand.

MAKES 10 TO 12 PARFAITS

2 McIntosh apples (about ½ pound, or 360 grams)

1 tablespoon (8g) cinnamon

1 tablespoon (16g) dark brown sugar

Pinch of salt

¼ cup (20g) chopped pecans

½ cup (45g) granola of your choice

3 cups (709ml) vanilla-flavored yogurt

Preheat the oven to 400°F. Peel and dice the apples into ¼- to ½-inch cubes. Place them in a medium microwave-safe bowl. Add the cinnamon, brown sugar, and salt. Microwave on high for 1 to 2 minutes, or until the apples are soft. Remove and set aside to cool, reserving any liquid in the bowl—as the apples cool, the liquid will thicken and become a syrup perfect for the parfait.

Spread the pecans out onto an ungreased baking sheet and toast them in the oven for 4 to 5 minutes, being careful not to burn the nuts. Mix the toasted pecans into the granola.

To assemble the parfaits, set out 10 to 12 small glass containers such as shot glasses or glass votive candle holders. Place about 1 teaspoon of the yogurt at the bottom of each container. Next, add 1 teaspoon of the apple mixture to each, then 1 teaspoon of the granola mix. Repeat the layers one more time. Transfer to the fridge and chill at least 1 hour before serving.

> Cinnamon is a common ingredient in love spells and can help spice up a romance. It has also been used for centuries in prosperity magic. Combined with pecans, which are associated with wealth and financial security, this recipe brings good luck in matters of the heart or the wallet.

ACKNOWLEDGMENTS

From both of us:

Joy Tutela, thank you for believing in us, and guiding us through every aspect, from seed to stem and leaf to bud, flower, and fruit.

Nina Shield, Lauren Appleton, Hannah Steigmeyer, Dorian Hastings, Laura Corless, Jess Morphew, Danielle Deschenes, Farin Schlussel, Carla Iannone, Marlena Brown, Marian Lizzi, Anne Kosmoski, Megan Newman, and the entire TarcherPerigee/Penguin Random House team, we are forever grateful for your collaboration. This book is better because of you. We also want to acknowledge Stella, who we feel played an important part in shaping its destiny.

June Jennings, thank you for your unwavering support at our events, and for your assistance with our teatime recipes.

Jennifer Iserloh, you are our favorite food alchemist. Thank you for breathing new life into our family formulas.

Lisa Ainsworth, your artwork brought our ideas to life. We are in awe of your talent. Thank you for saying yes.

Capricorn co-conspirator, career counselor, and consigliere Christian Day, you are the catalyst. A thousand thank-yous.

To the Gods!

∽

From Sandra:

Kevin, your support and love got me through all the trying times. You brought me into a famous author's family tree when you gave me a name to match my ambitions. All those Sundays we spent in the living room . . . you're holding the result in your hands. This, and my unending gratitude. Best. Husband. Ever.

Tara, my "red right hand," thank you for making the connection. Levi was right!

Li, my BFF and beta reader, you've been with me since the very beginning. Over the years, we have encouraged and inspired each other to write. It's your turn next!

Elphame, your energy and power transform lives. Deb, Leslie, and June: I am honored to call you my magickal family.

Brian Cain, walking the path and sharing the author's journey with you has been a pleasure. Blessed be.

To all the teachers who reassured me, and to the one professor who thought I couldn't write a book of poetry for my honors thesis because I didn't take her poetry course: you emboldened me. Thank you for laying the foundation I built my dreams on.

To all the industrious authors and warrior poets I have laughed and cried with: you get me! Many thanks.

I am grateful to Richard Ravish, who taught me that one intelligent person with a vision really could make a difference in the greater scheme of things—but, more important, to be mindful of what kind of difference. Richard always believed that life was far greater than any one person. He once told me, "Seventy years is a wink in the eye [of God]." I would not be the Witch I am, or the human being I am, if he had not mentored me, and the sadness I feel at his passing from the physical plane is lessened only by my conviction that Richard's sacred spirit lives on in his Great Work, as well as in the hearts of those who loved him. Azaradel, I hope I make you proud.

Leanne, thank you for the unstoppable force that is our friendship. I could have traveled the road alone, but it would not have been half as fun, and it would not be true to the magick of what we have wrought together for more than a decade. I can hardly wait for our next adventure!

"We're all here, and we're all safe."

꩜

From Leanne:

Elizabeth and Kevin, my children, who have inspired me with their imagination and passion for this lovely world. It has been an honor and privilege to be your mother. You keep me young and creative.

Acknowledgments

Chris Murphy, my love, my soul mate, and friend, you will always be my cup of tea. You are my person.

Auntie Lina, thank you for being there for me during my journey. From boys in blue shirts to wine at the tea events, you have always supported and joined me in my adventures.

To all my family who supported and encouraged me.

Shawn Poirier, thank you for the magic and the memories. This is all because I knew you.

Tim Reagan, thank you for illuminating my soul. You guided me to the light. May we always have laughter, wit, and wine. "A fo ben, bid bont."

My bard, Paul Orr, I am blessed to stand next to you in sacred space. Your radiant brow shines into the hearts of your magical family. May our magick continue to grow.

Coron Bendigedfran, thank you for sharing the journey with me.

My first magical family, Raven Moon, will always shine in my heart.

Lady Seren and Coron O'r Lleuadau, thank you for showing me the way. The bell will always be mine to ring.

Lady Faolan and Coron Nadroedd, I am blessed to have your support and love.

Lady Thalia and the Minoan Sisterhood, thank you for showing me the power and strength in the divine feminine.

To my Favorite, thank you for the hours of listening and support. You know who you are. May you sing with freedom in your soul.

Carol, you are the MVP. I will always be grateful for the times you calmed me down, and that time on the cruise when you emailed the signed documents for me.

Kelly, my darling, you are my sunshine; when we are together I feel fine. Kelly of mine! (The "Kelly Song" from *Cheers*.) Thank you for encouraging me through this process.

Remembering all my teachers at Shurtleff School and Revere High School. Thank you for feeding my creative soul.

Sandra, I will always be grateful for your support. Thank you for helping me find my crown. You are the power I needed in my life. We did it! The noise we made in the universe will always be heard.

GLOSSARY OF TEA LEAF SYMBOLS

Abbey—The appearance of an abbey in a reading is a sign of rising prosperity and luxury. There will be achievement and victory.

Acorn—An acorn in your cup is a good message. An acorn at the top of your cup means success, and at the bottom, good health.

Aircraft—Exciting things like travel by air or an elevation in career are coming to those who see an aircraft in their tea. The aircraft signifies soaring in the right direction for growth and rewards.

Albatross—The albatross is a premonition of sadness, sorrow, and death to sailors. If an albatross is perceived with the shape of a ship or water, it means bad travel at sea.

Alligator—Viewing an alligator means that there is possible danger around. People around you are causing anxiety and misery. A misfortune is impending.

Altar—For those who are religious, this indicates a time for prayers. It can also indicate that for those prayers to be answered, a sacrifice of some kind will be required. Give up something in the short term to gain something in the long term.

Anchor—Much like anchors on a boat, an anchor symbolizes stability in the difficult waves life throws at us.

Angels—Angels symbolically tell us good news is on the way. Sometimes a person will feel a deep connection to angelic forces, and seeing an angel in your cup can mean that the divine is speaking.

Antlers—A person with a strong life. Passion and sexual energy.

Ape—The ape in a reading warns you of fraud and anxiety. It reveals a stealthy enemy, and denotes malicious and dangerous people who talk behind your back.

Apple—Apples are not just gifts for teachers but also a reward for students and learners of all types. When an apple is found in your cup, knowledge, achievements, and accomplishments are forthcoming.

Arm—When an arm appears in a reading, love and happiness are with you. If the arm is bent, it means love that protects you with strength. If the arm is unfolded, new individuals will come into your life. These new influences bring affection and delight.

Armor—A knight's armor warns you of struggles and resentments on the horizon. You will need to protect yourself against the selfish actions of others.

Arrow—Traditional lore is loaded with meanings about arrows, and much of it is contradictory. It seems that arrows can mean so many things. They rely heavily on whatever else is in the cup to give a clear picture. In general, arrows pointing up are seen as favorable, and indicate that your perspective is accurate. Arrows pointing down indicate difficulties and cloudy judgment, with plans not working out unless you carefully reconsider your position.

Artichoke—Depression and melancholy are in your future if you see a symbol of an artichoke in your cup.

Awen—The Three Rays of Light. The Celtic word "Awen" means inspiration. It looks like three lines emanating down from a single point without touching. If you see this symbol, it means you will be inspired. Knowledge is coming. This can also mean luck.

Axe—The power to chop through to the heart of any issue. Difficulties will be cut down. A successful project or relationship.

Baby—As you might guess, a baby foretells a pregnancy. Also, babies can tell us of the formation of something new, like a business, a work of art, or some other project that we figuratively give birth to.

Bacon—A sign of good fortune, especially for a business. It indicates fat profits.

Ball—A ball in your tea leaves means you're about to successfully complete a task or a journey.

Balloon—A time to celebrate is coming. If the balloon is a hot air balloon, you will travel somewhere you've never been before.

Barn—A loving community will support you during a time of need. You have a strong circle you can count on.

Barrel—One barrel means a wonderful gathering of friends will be happening soon. If you see more than one barrel, it signifies that money is coming your way.

Basket—Your family will flourish. Gifts from friends will be arriving. Blessings abound.

Bat—A bat warns of unrewarding business ventures and failed projects. When you see a bat in your cup, you need to rethink your strategy. Don't rely on the way things look, because looks can be deceiving.

Bathtub—Regeneration and rebirth. This shape represents the cleansing of the soul. A fresh start.

Bean—This probably comes from the idea of "bean counting"; a bean symbolizes good fortune and monetary growth.

Bear—A bear can indicate extensive travel, particularly traveling north. Bears can also indicate a journey within.

Beaver—Hardworking and productive, beavers get things done. When a beaver shows up in the cup, a strong work ethic is indicated.

Bed—Beds represent rest and reflection. They also mean regeneration through love and peace.

Bee—Triumph and success through hard work. Bees are often a team of people who work together well. They also indicate that art such as poetry or music is influencing the spirit.

Bell—Surprise! Bells represent unexpected news. Depending on the symbols surrounding the bell in your cup, this can be a good or a bad omen.

Belt—A belt is a sign of protection and safety. Belts can also represent promises and commitments made.

Bicycle—Emotional and spiritual balance. Moving ahead during difficult times.

Birds—Birds are symbols of good news on the way. If the bird is a cardinal, it can also mean a message from the dead.

Boat—Seeing a boat in your cup means travel, and not just on a cruise. Depending on the surrounding images, boats can also mean a visit from a companion.

Bone—A bone in the reading instructs a person to stay focused on a task. Presence of a bone tells a person that strength and resolution are needed to move forward.

Book—Books are symbols of knowledge and revelation of secret knowledge. Educational endeavors are on the horizon.

Boot—Moving ahead, walking into a new situation. An exciting change in career or love.

Bottle—Great awareness inspires your choices and guides you as you chart the course of your life. Knowledge is nourishment to your soul. Delve deeper into your interests.

Bouquet of flowers—Love, peace, and beauty coming to a person's life.

Bow (and arrow)—Anxiety about choices on the horizon. This is a time of tension and stress, but it is also an opportunity to take careful aim at your goals before taking action.

Bowl—A full bowl in a reading is a blessing. When your bowl is full, you will enjoy wealth and be lucky in love. An empty bowl signifies progress in many aspects of life: spiritual, material, and interpersonal growth.

Box—A box means there is something secret you must protect. Keep your confidences.

Branch—A branch indicates a flexible, easy-going person. It predicts success in love and life in general. It can also herald a time of great joy. In a health reading, a branch indicates a return to wellness.

Bread—Celebrate the little things. Pay attention to what gives love and sustenance every day.

Bridge—The bridge predicts the passing from difficulty to peace.

Despite a period of strife and trouble, a new chapter of life will begin, and happiness can be found.

Broom—A time to sweep away the old, and usher in the new. Brush off criticism, and clear away negativity.

Brush (hairbrush)—A warning that you must clean up your spiritual life and remove the people causing knots and snarls in your personal journey.

Brush (paintbrush)—Creative ventures bring fulfillment. There are many ways to be artistic. Explore ideas for decorating, or take a class in something fun that will allow you to express yourself.

Buffalo—The help you have been waiting for is coming. Buffalos denote a time of rejuvenation.

Building—Seeing this structure in your tea leaves indicates dreams becoming reality.

Bull—The bull represents power, strength, and vitality. This is an indicator of good health.

Butterfly—A powerful symbol of transformation and change, the greatest of which is death. In many cultures, butterflies are considered messages from the dead. Seeing two butterflies in the cup means love is on the way to you.

Button—This humble item has a prominent job: holding things together. The button represents a strong commitment.

Cabbage—This symbol has traditionally indicated poverty. If you see a cabbage in your tea leaves, you need to take a serious look at your bills, your investments, and your long-term financial plan.

Cabinet—The shape of a cabinet indicates assets, financial security, and long-term wealth.

Cakes—People who see cakes in their readings will soon have busy social calendars. Cakes imply new friends, parties, and special occasions.

Candle—Viewing a candle in your tea leaf reading means sacred light surrounds you. Look to those around you for guidance. If you are experiencing a dark time, this is a beacon of hope.

Canoe—Canoes in readings symbolize new interactions that will turn into long-term relationships.

Carnations—These humble but beautiful flowers have genuine staying power. Honest and loyal friends and lovers bring joy when carnations are seen in the cup.

Casket—Time for deep meditation and reflection. Someone is giving you wisdom from beyond the grave. Pay close attention to the other symbols in the cup.

Castle—Luxury, excess, and extravagance. An omen of an inheritance or an unexpected gift.

Cat—Traditionally, the cat has been interpreted as a symbol of deception, cruelty, and arguments between friends. When the tea leaves show a cat jumping, prepare yourself for financial problems.

Cauldron—A cauldron is a symbol of rebirth and magic. When there is a cauldron in your reading, watch for wonderful new opportunities that you can cook up into successful ventures with a bit of time and attention.

Chain—A chain in the tea leaves can have many different meanings. Take careful note of the surrounding images, as they will help decipher the message. A chain can mean DNA: biological links that contain important information, particularly where health is concerned. The chain can also indicate an engagement and an eventual wedding, if the chain is well-formed. It is a symbol that reminds us to pay attention to the way things link up in our world. Focus on connections.

Chair—A chair in the cup means a guest is coming; the type of guest is revealed by the nearby symbols.

Cheese—Cheese is a positive symbol. Cheese in a reading means colleagues of influence will help you monetarily and guide you on a career path.

Cherries—Cherries signify an arrival of a lover or new friends.

Christmas tree—Christmas trees are a celebration of life and family. For matters of timing, they represent winter.

Circle—The unbroken shape of a circle in your leaves means triumph and completion. (If the circle is incomplete, there is more work to be done in order to attain your goal. It is time to revise your strategy.)

Clock—A clock in the cup is a great message for your health. It indicates the gift of more time to enjoy life.

Clover—The clover is a wonderful missive that announces good luck and fortune.

Coins—Coins are a measure of financial status. If the coin is at the top of the cup, money is coming in. At the bottom of the cup, money is flowing out, so be sure to watch your spending.

Comet—When a comet is streaking across your cup, great news is on the way.

Condom—If the shape of a condom appears in the tea leaves, be cautious of your own health and the emotional energy of those around you.

Corn—Corn represents fertility and wealth.

Cow—A cow means successful and serene days are ahead for the seeker.

Crab—This is the astrological symbol of Cancer, and Cancerians are known for being moody and emotional. A crab in your reading can indicate crabby people, so be mindful of your reactions when dealing with the outbursts of others. A large crab is a red flag: beware of an enemy waiting to pinch you.

Crescent moon—Emotions are warm and loving when the crescent moon shines in a cup. Dreams are coming true.

Cross—When we protect ourselves or those we love, it can come at a cost. A cross in the tea leaves is a message of defense or sacrifice.

Crown—A portent of rewards to come, the crown indicates recognition and prestige. When the crown can be seen on a head, it means you have mastered a skill.

Crystal—Psychic abilities and prophetic messages coming from the great beyond.

Cube—Constancy and understanding will transpire between friends and coworkers.

Cup—A cup in your tea leaves means a great reward is coming. The cup has long been regarded as a symbol of rewards in love. When doing a mediumship reading, this is a message of love from those you miss the most.

Daffodils—These flowers can mean that an event you have waited for is about to happen. Depending on the symbols around them, they may indicate travel with close friends.

Dagger—Daggers are symbols of power, but take heed, they are also warnings. A dagger cautions of danger. The symbols around the dagger will help define the nature of the danger.

Dahlias—Dahlias denote events occurring in the fall, and can represent an increase in finances, particularly through wise investments and saving.

Daisies—Seeing a daisy in the cup declares that the seeker is a person filled with joy and happiness and shares it with all those around them.

Dancers—The manifestation of dancers in your cup represents good news and happiness.

Deer—A deer in a reading is a warning that if there is no change on a current professional path, a career will end in ruin. If the deer is racing, past mistakes will not be corrected.

Devil—Be aware of people acting on their basic animalistic instincts. The devil is a symbol of control and can indicate addiction issues.

Dish—Seeing a dish in your cup reveals stress and anxiety in the home. When the dish is broken, be forewarned: family life is falling apart.

Dog—For centuries, humankind's best friend has been a symbol of loyalty and unconditional love of family and friends. If the dog is surrounded by negative symbols, a romantic relationship is at risk of ending.

Doll—The image of a doll represents someone hiding their feelings.

Dolphin—Dolphins can mean travel by water: a trip on a boat, a ferry, or even a cruise. It can also indicate a person with a happy, positive outlook on life.

Door—Doors found in a teacup have different meanings depending on the position of the door. If the door is opening, it means something new is coming. If the door is closed, it represents old issues and relationships coming to an end.

Dove—Doves predict the arrival of a romantic partner. Doves within a tea leaf reading can also confirm that loving friends and family are around you.

Dragon—The dragon cautions against hasty changes. Dragons are a symbol of wise counsel and protection, so when you see a dragon in your cup, take the time to carefully consider your options before taking action. Many witches see dragons as a symbol of power and strength; in a reading about health, this is a sign of vitality and longevity.

Dragonfly—Dragonflies indicate new adventures ahead. They have been linked to fairies and magic, and some people believe they bring messages from those who have crossed over.

Duck—As the saying goes, "Get your ducks in a row." When you see a duck in your cup, your finances will be sorted out. Stability and security follow.

Dumbbell—Dumbbells suggest that new friends are on the horizon.

Dust pan and brush—When a dust pan and a brush are viewed in the tea leaves, there will be fights and arguments with family or partners.

Egg—Eggs represent creation and new beginnings. They are one of the symbols that can predict pregnancy.

Elephant—This lovable pachyderm predicts wisdom, strength, and luck.

Envelope—The appearance of an envelope represents a message coming. This message can be either positive or negative, depending on the surrounding symbols.

Eye—When you spy with your little eye an eye in your tea leaves, it can have two different messages depending on if the eye is open or closed. Open, it forecasts an awakening in your life. New information is being revealed. Closed, it means information that is yet to be seen. Something may be purposefully hidden. Examine other symbols close by for clues.

Face—If the face is happy, a lover or new friend is coming. Seeing an unhappy face means someone is not faithful to you.

Fan—A fan means someone is hiding romantic feelings.

Feather—Feathers are messages from spirit, whether they are seen within a teacup or simply discovered in nature. They can also imply that the seeker is rising up, doing better in life.

Fence—Fences signify limitations, obstacles, or boundaries. They can sometimes indicate minor setbacks, but they are not cause for alarm. Any delays will be temporary.

Fire—Fire has different meanings in a tea leaf reading depending on where it appears. At the top, it signifies that you are about to achieve something great. Find fire at the bottom of the cup, and your haste will have you in danger.

Fireworks—A celebration is coming in the future. Exciting success is coming to a career.

Fish—A fish in the cup predicts good fortune; if the fish appears to be dead, however, then it is a warning of the loss of money.

Fly—Flies are pests. Beware of an annoyance coming into your home life.

Fork—When the leaves form a fork, watch out! Forks stand for false flattery and two-faced people.

Forked line—Seeing a forked line in the cup means it is time to make decisions.

Fruit—In general, fruit represents a bounty of blessings coming into your life.

Gallows—This is a bad omen. The gallows can indicate court battles.

Garland—A positive symbol of joy, love, and respect.

Gate—Opportunities arise that put you on the path of success.

Geese—A group of these aggressive migrators indicates the arrival of difficult houseguests. (For just one, see the entry for *Goose*.)

Giraffe—Giraffes caution against careless mistakes. To avoid trouble, speak with care and knowledge before giving information.

Glass—Seeing a glass means good times with great friends are forthcoming.

Goat—Traditionally, the shape of a goat was interpreted to be a warning of enemies working against the seeker. The goat is associated with fierce independence and the ability to scale treacherous heights, so when you see the goat, it is time to rise above the petty behaviors of others.

Goose—A single goose foretells travel that will require detailed arrangements. If planning isn't handled carefully, the trip will be canceled.

Grapes—Grapes are a hopeful message indicating a future filled with richness and indulgence.

Grasshoppers—Grasshoppers are omens for declining business and financial growth. This is also a warning of disease.

Grave—The image of a grave is a message of death. Sadness is coming to friends and family. When this shows up while you are doing mediumship with the tea leaves, someone from the grave is sending advice to the living.

The Green Man—The Green Man is depicted as a foliate head, or face of a man surrounded by leaves, and represents lushness, abundance, and fertility. For questions of timing, the Green Man equates to summer.

Guitar—A guitar is a passionate message of a deep sexual attraction. The person who is attracted to the seeker will be met during travel.

Gun—The image of a gun with no other negative symbols around it indicates sex and passion. When shown with undesirable images, the gun is a warning of explosive reactions and dangerous situations.

Hammer—The presence of a hammer in the tea leaves indicates hard work is needed. It can mean the need to express yourself. The seeker may have to hammer home a point or idea more aggressively.

Hammock—A hammock is a warning that something that was anticipated will fail. To avoid disappointment, look at the other symbols for advice.

Hand—The presence of a hand in the cup has two different meanings, depending on whether the hand is open or closed. Open, it means the joys of friendship. Closed, it means an argument.

Handcuffs—When handcuffs appear in the tea leaves, legal issues that lead to jail time are looming in the future. Trust your instincts when you feel someone around you is shady.

Hare—Hares can be distinguished in a reading from a rabbit due to their large size. This is a message of an absent friend returning to your life. If the hare is running, travel is ahead.

Harp—A harp symbolizes love and harmony. If you are uncertain about how others feel about you, seeing this message in the cup means you are well loved.

Hat—A hat in your cup is a message about consciousness, symbolizing an awareness coming to you. Hats also speak about compassion, for others as well as the self.

Hawk—A hawk flying in your teacup is a warning about jealousy; you may have jealous people around you, depending on the other images you see. You may also be the jealous one. The hawk signals an invitation to do some soul-searching and confront your feelings.

Heart—The shape of a heart in the tea leaves is usually a beautiful message. Hearts represent pleasure, love, trust, and compassion. If you see an anatomical heart, the shape of a heart near medical symbols, or if this is a question regarding health, the heart should be regarded as a reminder to take good care of yourself and to check in with your doctor.

Hen—A hen in your cup predicts a coming pregnancy.

Horse—If you see an image of a horse galloping in your cup, it means good news. The head of a horse in the leaves means the arrival of a lover.

Horseshoe—When a horseshoe appears in your cup with its ends toward the rim, it means good luck is around you. With the ends toward the bottom, it reveals that someone is attracted to you.

Hourglass—If you see an hourglass in your cup, it means time is running out. A choice needs to be made quickly. Act swiftly to avoid loss.

House—The shape of a house in your cup means you are secure. If you are facing changes, you can proceed with confidence of success.

Initials—If you recognize the initials and they are those of someone you know, the other symbols in the cup will clarify the message and how that person is involved. If you recognize the initials, and they are those of a loved one who has crossed over, the other symbols in the cup will contain a message for you from that person. If you do not recognize them, they are someone who will play a key role in the future, so watch for them. If they appear next to symbols of love, they are a future romantic interest.

Iron (appliance)—An iron flattens out the wrinkles in clothing. Irons represent the termination of troubles and a smoother future ahead. A quarrel comes to an end.

Ivy—Supportive and faithful friends and family are there for you, cheering you on.

Jar—A bounty of goodness will soon arrive.

Jewels—These treasures remind us to count our blessings. This is a time to examine what you have to be thankful for and focus on the good things in your life. Cultivate an attitude of gratitude, and realize that you have what you need.

Jug—Party time! A celebration is in the works.

Jupiter—The symbol of the planet Jupiter— ♃ —is a wonderful omen. It heralds luck and abundance to the seeker. This planet symbolizes great good fortune, the favor of people in high places, and status.

Kangaroo—A kangaroo hopping into your reading means there is security and harmony in the home.

Kite—The presence of a kite in the leaves means freedom. Wishes and dreams are coming true.

Knife—When reading your leaves and the unfortunate image of a knife appears, it means friendships will be cut. Beware of a hidden enemy.

Ladder—A ladder indicates that a job promotion is forthcoming. Hard work pays off, and the seeker is climbing the ranks.

Lamb—A lamb in a reading is a sign that the seeker will start a very daring project that will be successful.

Lamp—At the top of the cup, a lamp means a feast and rewards are arriving soon. When at the side of the cup, it means secrets around you will be revealed. When the lamp is at the bottom of the cup, something will be postponed.

Leaf—The symbol of a leaf in your tea leaves means new life and new beginnings.

Lines—Lines formed by the tea leaves represent distinctive changes in the progress of your life. If the lines are straight, it means advancement, improvement, and growth. If the lines are wavy, your path is uncertain. More focus and greater effort are required to move forward successfully.

Lion—The feline embodiment of courage and strength is also the astrological symbol of Leo. The appearance of a lion in your leaves means gaining control and closure in difficult situations. A lion near the top of the cup means influential friends will support you.

Lock—The appearance of a closed lock within a tea leaf reading denotes obstacles in your path. If the lock appears open, new information is unfolding.

Loop—Loops are symbols of time and creation. They are warnings against impulsive actions.

Man—When a man is seen in the tea leaves, a specific masculine person may be indicated, based on what you see in the symbols surrounding him. If you are doing mediumship, the man can indicate a loved one. If the reading is of a general nature, the condition of the man is a metaphor for the state of your concern. If the man appears large, there is bounty and wealth. If the man appears youthful, success and good fortune are on the way. If the man appears crooked, hunched over, or scrawny, lean times are ahead.

Mask—Illusions, hidden information, and subterfuge are indicated by the image of a mask. Take extra care in your dealings.

Mountain—Sometimes the image of a mountain is simply a location that is specific to the seeker; if there is a specific place that holds meaning and the other symbols coincide, then the mountain indicates the significance of the location. If there is no personal context for a mountain, it indicates the challenges that will be faced. Look to the nearby symbols for ways to overcome obstacles and attain your goals.

Mouse—A mouse is a warning of theft. Take extra care to protect what you believe is precious in your life. In today's world, a mouse is also commonly associated with a computer, so this can mean connections made online.

Mushroom—Mushrooms seen at the top of the cup mean a journey or a dramatic move to another country; at the bottom of the cup, rapid growth.

Nail—A warning of unfair treatment and a lack of justice.

Necklace—If it is broken, it means a relationship will end. Unbroken, it signifies admirers around the seeker.

Needle—The image of a needle in the cup metaphorically means recognition and admiration, but the needle can also represent sewing or weaving. Someone who enjoyed sewing in life could be reaching out from the grave. Seeing more than one needle can mean frustration in a romantic relationship.

Net—Good times are coming after a period of stress and chaos.

Nose—If the nose is twisted, proceed with caution: an untrustworthy person is near. If the nose is slim, life is changing. A large and swollen nose indicates overindulgence in food, drink, or both.

Nurse—If a nurse is seen in the cup and no one in the family is or was a nurse, the seeker should check in with a doctor.

Nuts—Hard work will be rewarded with an increase in wealth.

Oak—The mighty oak tree is a sign of long life and good health. It can also indicate a milestone in the journey to self-discovery.

Oar—A complete oar means fun and merriment will be forthcoming. If the oar is broken or bent, irresponsibility leads to bad luck.

Onions—Onions reveal the hidden plans of disloyal friends.

Orchids—Orchids are lovely flowers that foretell a brilliant future filled with abundance and peace.

Ostrich—When this odd bird appears near the bottom of the cup, travel is in your future. When it falls near the handle, you are deliberately ignoring the truth in a situation.

Owl—The wise owl issues a warning in a reading: avoid gossip, don't trust people who suddenly want to be close to you, and look beyond the surface to understand what's really going on.

Ox—An ox is a positive indicator of peace, richness, and love around the home and family.

Oysters—Near the handle, oysters are a sign that you have extravagant tastes. At the bottom of the cup, oysters predict that as the seeker gets older, life will get better.

Palm tree—Depending on the surrounding symbolism, palm trees can suggest the tropics and the beautiful places palm trees grow. At the bottom of the cup, palm trees forecast success and honor.

Parrot—Parrots can represent stories that are repeated, or empty talk. With regard to pregnancy, parrots predict twins.

Pig—The shape of a pig indicates greed. The surrounding symbols will reveal the source.

Purse—A purse near the rim means profit in business. At the bottom, it represents a loss in revenue.

Queen—A queen on her throne specifies nobility and harmony. Respect and acknowledgment will be achieved.

Question mark—The question mark is an emblem of the unknown. Use caution when embarking on new journeys or dealings.

Quill pen—A quill represents legal documents that will be signed. Depending on the surrounding images, it can indicate a marriage.

Rabbit—Rabbits are often a sign of fertility, but they can have other meanings depending on the nature of the questions asked. A rabbit can indicate a need for bravery. Near the handle, they indicate anxiety. At the bottom of the cup, a rabbit is a sign of good luck in the future.

Rake—"You reap what you sow." The rake can indicate the concept of karma. The rake is related to planting seeds of spiritual and earthly growth.

Raven—Ravens are traditionally regarded as the bearers of bad news in a tea leaf reading because they are associated with death. They signify endings, and making way for new beginnings.

Ring—A ring can indicate a number of things: something specific, such as a meaningful phone call, or if it is really large, it can indicate a broader concept like your life coming full circle, or returning to your roots. If the ring is at the top of the cup, it means an offer of marriage. If it is at the bottom of the cup, it means a long engagement. If the ring is broken, it means a promise will be broken, or an engagement will be called off.

Rose—Rose is the flower of life. If the seeker is looking to know about future children, it represents bloodlines and creation. If the person getting the reading is asking questions about future romance, this is a great omen. The rose predicts the arrival of a powerful love.

Saturn—Seeing the symbol for the planet Saturn in your cup can mean it's time to fortify your boundaries and keep negative people out of your inner circle. Saturn signifies power and influence, as well as discipline. If you want to make changes in your life, the symbol of Saturn in your tea leaves is a sign that now is the time.

Saw—A saw means a parting of ways between friends. A relationship is plagued by interference. There are times when it is necessary to let someone go.

Scale—Scales in a reading denote legal issues. If the scales appear balanced, it means that legal issues will be solved in a just manner. If the scales are unbalanced, it is telling you that the result will be unjustified.

Scissors—Scissors in a reading are signals that there are quarrels on the horizon. These disagreements can lead to a separation between lovers, business partners, or friends.

Sheep—When there are sheep in your cup, it means good fortune will come to you.

Shell—A shell is a lovely message of good news arriving.

Shoe—Shoes have soles, people have souls. When you have a shoe in your reading, pay attention to the condition of the bottom of the shoe. If the sole appears damaged or broken, then the soul of the seeker is in need of care. If the sole of the shoe is well-formed, then the soul of the seeker is healthy and happy.

Snake—Snakes are powerful images for magical people. When a snake materializes in a reading, it means wisdom. If the snake is in an attack pose, then it indicates an enemy. Outwit the rival with wisdom.

Spider—When the spider chooses to emerge in a reading, it is time to cooperate with others to achieve a goal. Spiders remind us that joining forces to form a web is a powerful way to accomplish your objectives.

Star—Stars of any number of points are a message of health and happiness to all who are blessed to receive them in their reading. The star denotes hope. When working with mediumship in the cup, it is a sign of communication from the afterlife.

Stork—A stork indicates that a baby will be arriving into the life of

the seeker. It can also be the "birth" of new beginnings, a fresh outlook, or the arrival of a loving relationship.

Sun—The sun is a portent of contentment, victory, and dominance.
Its warmth and positive strength softens any negative symbols in
the cup.

Sword—If you recognize a sword among your tea leaves, it's time to
prepare for an argument. The environment breeds disagreements and
opposition. Don't let emotions get to you. The sword indicates that
the best way to combat this is to rely on solid logic and reason.

Table—Time to get a date book! Seeing a table in a reading means
that there will be many social engagements forthcoming. Tables
remind the inquirer to think outside of the box.

Tambourine—Tambourines mean that an announcement that a person has been waiting for is arriving soon. A tambourine is an indica-
tion of joy after a difficult and stressful time.

Tea cozy—If you are single, a tea cozy suggests that a relationship will
be arriving. If you are married and see a tea cozy, your relationship is
strong and filled with love.

Teacup and saucer—The image of the cup and saucer is a broad message that the current reading is going to be good.

Teeth—When you see teeth in a tea leaf reading, it's time to visit the dentist. (For just one, see the entry for Tooth.)

Telephone—When a telephone is in a cup, the ringing is an alarm to advise you to pay attention to avoid problems due to carelessness. It could also be a call from the other side.

Tent—A tent in a reading implies that you should cover your ass and protect yourself; it can indicate that someone is hiding the truth. If the seeker enjoys the great outdoors, it is a sign that it is a good time to plan a travel adventure.

Thimble—A thimble informs the inquirer that there will be changes in their home.

Throne—A person sitting on a throne is a message of promotion and success, but if the throne is empty, it warns of an embarrassment in a community.

Thumb—A huge thumb seen in the tea leaves predicts the opportunity to redeem yourself to people who dislike you.

Tiger—A tiger indicates trouble and carelessness on the part of your associates.

Toad—Unfavorable truths will be exposed when toads are in your cup. This is an omen of liars among friends and the division of loyalties.

Tongue—Wagging tongues can hurt friends. The image of a tongue represents a person who has spoken ill of a friend. This is a warning of causing pain with unkind words. Speak with care, and old wounds will heal and new friendships will flourish.

Tooth—When one tooth appears in a reading, grief and sorrow will follow.

Torch—A burning torch indicates hope and individual discovery. It illuminates hidden talents and gifts that will bring wealth and success to the seeker.

Tortoise—A beneficial form of criticism is coming to the seeker. The tortoise indicates a time of slow progress. Have patience. Slow and steady wins the race. (If your shape has short, stubby legs and looks like it is walking on the ground, it's a tortoise. If the legs are out to the sides like it is swimming, it's a turtle.)

Train—Trains predict travel as well as the metaphor of arriving at a wonderful point in your life.

Tree—Trees suggest improvements in life. It is a representation of life itself and creation. A tree informs you of a clear path opening up. Good health and family growth are indicated.

Triangle—If a triangle appears within a reading, unexpected complications may arise. The triangle can also represent three people in a relationship that will end in conflict.

Trident—Associated with Poseidon, ruler of the sea, the trident is a special message of promotion to those in the navy or working on the ocean. The trident denotes honor and respect.

The triquetra—The triquetra is a symbol created by a single line that weaves within itself. This is the symbol for the spirit that never dies. This can be confirmation of communication with someone who has crossed over.

Trumpet—The trumpet loudly announces good news for performers, especially musicians. This instrument will predict new business adventures and social engagements.

Trunk—The suitcase, or "trunk" as it was traditionally named, indicates a change in surroundings: new people enter, and some people who do not add value depart.

Tub—An old-fashioned, round hand-washing tub is a warning to choose your associates wisely; you may turn up some dirt about someone in your circle.

Tulips—The appearance of tulips mean friends are loving and filled with trustworthiness. They are also a sign of strength in readings relating to health.

Turkey—When you see a turkey in your tea leaves, it's time to stop goofing around and get serious.

Turtle—This slow mover indicates a stable home, good fortune, and luxuries. A turtle is an affirmation that someone's home is secure and protected. (If your shape has short, stubby legs and looks like it is walking on the ground, it's a tortoise. If the legs are out to the sides like it is swimming, it's a turtle.)

Twins (two stick figures)—Seeing twins means a family will soon have double the fun. Twins are messages of joy to all who are gifted with their image.

UFO—The shape of an unidentified flying object (flying saucer shape) is a sign of psychic ability. It may be time to meditate and communicate with your higher self.

Umbrella—When the umbrella is open, a bad weather forecast and irritations are coming. If the umbrella is closed, bad luck can be avoided if attention is paid to the surrounding situation.

Undergarments—Underwear or undergarments represent revealing someone's true nature. Sexual attraction.

Unicorn—The fun and fantastical symbol of a unicorn is cautionary of scandals heading into a person's life.

Urn—The symbol of the urn signifies that conflicting definitions will be discovered. When coupled with positive symbols, the urn signifies abundance and contentment to the seeker. The urn has been known to predict illness, or indicate messages from the dead in the cup. Pay attention to the surrounding symbols.

Valley—Deep and personal matters are being considered. A person of strong spiritual integrity.

Vampire—Seeing the visage of a vampire in the tea leaves means sorrow is going to suck the joy from your life. Rarely, it can predict the death of someone close to you.

Van—This vehicle is a sign that a new adventure will drive you to success.

Vase—A vase is a warning that a friend needs help. If nearby symbols are positive, the vase is a message of good health.

Venus—The planetary symbol, which is also the symbol for woman— ♀—denotes a time of peace and love in the seeker's life.

Violets—More than one violet in the reading means joyful days are ahead. If the violets form the shape of a cross, beware: poor health and possible death. More often, violets are symbols of delight.

Volcano—Usually the person who sees a volcano needs to relieve stress and find ways to express themselves before they blow up.

Vulture—Vultures bring messages of sorrow, grief, and regret. An enemy is winning, and the seeker will lose a great deal over time. Vultures can be a warning of issues on a global scale.

Wagon—The appearance of a wagon in a reading foretells a wedding.

Walking stick—A walking stick is a reminder to notice the changes that have occurred, and be mindful of the passage of time. Wisdom will come to the seeker through a shift in perspective.

Wall—Walls represent complications and problems in the future. Bravery and vigor will be needed in order to create the change necessary to conquer the obstacles.

Wasp—The nasty wasp gives the seeker a warning of romantic problems.

Waterfall—A waterfall is a prophecy of success and prosperity.

Whale—The mighty whale is a symbol of the unknown. Whales symbolize fear and confusion before reaching a new destiny. If you trust your instinct and stay on your path, you will find treasures.

Wheel—Wheels have two opposite meanings in a tea leaf reading. If the wheel is broken, it means disappointment. If the wheel is whole, it means good fortune.

Wheelbarrow—A responsible, helpful person, a person whose purpose is being of service to others.

Window—Seeing life from a new point of view. A window indicates a personal awakening.

Wineglass—Cheers! A wineglass is an image of celebration and friendship.

Wings—Wings can be a powerful message from the beyond. Those who have crossed over often send us wings to let us know they are around. Angel wings indicate blessings and a "guardian angel" watching over you. In general, wings of any kind can suggest hope and travel.

Wishbone—If a wishbone is seen in the cup, make a wish!

Witch—A witch is a symbol of power, often a power that is fearsome to the willfully ignorant.

Wizard—A wizard in the tea leaves is a sign of enchantment, or supernatural activity.

Wolf—When a wolf appears with negative symbols, be forewarned that jealous people are close by. Keep your guard up. When the wolf shows up with positive symbols, you have found your tribe. You will have each other's backs in times of trouble.

Woman—When a woman is seen in the tea leaves, a specific feminine person may be indicated, based on what you see in the symbols surrounding her. If you are doing mediumship, the woman can indicate a loved one. If the reading is of a general nature, the condition of the woman is a metaphor for the state of your concern. If the woman appears large, there is bounty and wealth. If the woman appears youthful, success and good fortune are on the way. If the woman appears crooked, hunched over, or scrawny, lean times are ahead.

Wreath—Depending on the surrounding images and the seeker's intention, a wreath can mean a celebration of life or good fortune. If the images surrounding the wreath are dark and foreboding, this is a message of sorrow and loss.

Yacht—A yacht is a sign of abundance and contentment for the future.

Yew tree—A yew tree can symbolize an inheritance, a reward, or promotion at work, or an increase in social status, depending on the symbols it appears with.

Yoke—A yoke (the wooden harness that fastens two animals to a wagon or plow) is a symbol that implies command and domination play a role in the situation. Be wary of control issues.

Zebra—Zebra is usually a fun indicator of a voyage ahead, often to exotic places far away. If the other symbols in the cup indicate quarrels or disagreements, the zebra indicates that the issues are polarizing, and the resolution leaves no room for half measures.

Zero—Zero means it is time to meditate and slow down before proceeding with a project. Rather than seeing it as "nothing," imagine the zero expressing pure potential, and the wide-open possibilities that lie ahead.

BIBLIOGRAPHY

"A Basic List of Tea Leaf Symbols." The Mystic Tea Room, http://www.mystic tearoom.com/wiki/A_Basic_List_of_Tea_Leaf_Symbols.

"A Dictionary of Symbols." Divination of Tea Leaves, http://www.divination bytealeaves.com/a-dictionary-of-symbols-a.htm.

"Alchemical Properties of Foods: Hundreds of Foodstuffs Classified According to Their Elemental Nature." AlchemyLab.com, https://www.alchemylab .com/guideto.htm.

Cabot, Laurie, and Tom Cowan. *Power of the Witch: The Earth, the Moon, and the Magical Path to Enlightenment*. New York: Delta, 1990.

"Cascarilla Powder." The Witchipedia, http://www.witchipedia.com/def :cascarilla-powder.

"Common Meanings & Symbols Found in Tea Leaf Readings." Best Online Psychics, May 11, 2017, https://www.bestonlinepsychics.net/psychic-info /tea-leaf-readings/.

Delorme, Jules, et al. "Salmon Symbolism." Spirit Animal Totems, October 6, 2018, https://www.spirit-animals.com/salmon-symbolism/.

Goodwin, Lindsey. "Tasseography Symbols for Reading Coffee or Tea Leaves" The Spruce Eats, August 14, 2019, https://www.thespruceeats.com/tasseog raphy-tea-leaf-reading-symbols-765838.

Heiss, Mary Lou, and Robert J. Heiss. *The Story of Tea: A Cultural History and Drinking Guide*. Berkeley, CA: Ten Speed Press, 2007.

"Herb/Plant—Sugar Cane." *Information and Correspondents in Witchcraft*, February 21, 2015, https://vayas-witchcraft-and-spiritual.tumblr.com/post/111650185765/herbplant-sugar-cane.

Hoh, Erling, and Victor H. Mair. *The True History of Tea*. New York: Thames & Hudson, 2009.

"How to Read Tea Leaves: A Beginner's Guide to Tea Leaf Symbols and Meanings." Psychic Gurus, https://www.psychicgurus.org/how-to-read-tea-leaves/.

Moone, Aurora. "Magickal Correspondences of Dill." Plentiful Earth, February 6, 2018, https://plentifulearth.com/magickal-correspondences-dill/.

Patterson, Rachel. *A Kitchen Witch's World of Magical Food*. Hants, England: Moon Books, 2015.

Picard, Caroline. "25 Fall Flowers That'll Spruce Up Your Garden This Autumn." *Good Housekeeping*, July 10, 2019, https://www.goodhousekeeping.com/home/gardening/g22563541/fall-flowers/.

Silva, Jose, with Philip Miele. *The Silva Mind Control Method*. New York: Pocket Books, 1991.

"Tea Leaf Dictionary." Auntyflo.com, https://www.auntyflo.com/tea-leaf-dictionary.

"Top 10 Autumn and Winter-Flowering Bulbs." Thompson & Morgan, https://www.thompson-morgan.com/top-10-autumn-winter-flowering-bulbs.

Wigington, Patti. "Salt Folklore and Magic: Using Salt in Modern Pagan Traditions." Learn Religions, April 2, 2018, https://www.learnreligions.com/salt-folklore-and-magic-2562502.

ABOUT THE AUTHORS

Sandra Mariah Wright is a prominent Salem Witch and the High Priestess of Elphame, an Alexandrian coven, and its outer court group, Gallows Hill Grove. She lives with her husband; their pug, Abigail; and their two magickal kitties, Merlin and Marie Marie, on her family's estate on Gallows Hill in Salem, where nineteen people were hanged for the charge of Witchcraft.

Sandra owns an events business, Spirit Beacon Psychic Fair & Mystical Marketplace, as well as a jewelry and occult supply company, Gallows Hill Witchery, and manages the largest annual psychic fair in the country. She has appeared on the Travel Channel and Showtime, and has been featured on Dish Network's *Magnificent Obsessions*.

Leanne Marrama is a renowned Salem Witch, full-time professional psychic, and High Priestess in the Celtic Traditionalist Gwyddonaid as well as The Minoan Sisterhood. She teaches classes, presents at festivals around the country, and hosts weekly séances in Salem. Among her many media appearances, she has been featured on TLC's

What Not to Wear, *Beyond Belief with George Noory*, and also on the History channel.

On the first Thursday of every month, Leanne and Sandra host *The Psychic Tea*, a radio show on 102.9FM HD2 that is also broadcast live on their Facebook page, The Psychic Teas. All previous shows can be replayed from the archive on that page.